Vampire Readings

An Annotated Bibliography

Patricia Altner

Illustrations by Joan Temo

The Scarecrow Press, Inc.
Lanham, Maryland, & London

SCARECROW PRESS, INC.

Published in the United States of America
by Scarecrow Press, Inc.
4720 Boston Way
Lanham, Maryland 20706

4 Pleydell Gardens, Folkestone
Kent CT20 2DN, England

Copyright © 1998 by Patricia Altner

British Library Cataloguing in Publication Information Available

Library of Congress Cataloging-in-Publication Data

Altner, Patricia, 1948– .
    Vampire readings : an annotated bibliography / Patricia Altner ;
illustrations by Joan Temo.
        p.   cm.
    Includes bibliographical references and index.
    ISBN 0-8108-3504-5 (pbk. : alk. paper)
    1. Vampires in literature—Bibliography.   2. Fiction—20th
century —Bibliography.   3. Vampires—Bibliography.   I. Title.
Z6514.C5V352   1998
016.8088′0375—dc21   98-33693
                                                                    CIP

♾ ™The paper used in this publication meets the minimum require-
ments of American National Standard for Information Sciences—Per-
manence of Paper for Printed Library Materials, ANSI Z39.48–1984.
Manufactured in the United States of America.

To my guys and my mom

CONTENTS

ACKNOWLEDGMENTS

My thanks to:

Cathy Krusberg—known to Internet subscribers of the vampyres discussion list as the Mad Bibliographer. Cathy is also the reviewer for the fanzine "Vampire Crypt." She has generously shared her extensive knowledge of vampire literature.

Thomas Ofcansky—scholar and vampire enthusiast. He gave the manuscript a careful reading and me hints on how to make it better.

Ellen Rawlings—mystery writer (*Deadly Harvest* [Fawcett, 1997] is her latest) and volunteer reader and editor. She said she only performed this onerous task because I am a friend. I appreciate that.

Cynthia Parker—bookseller. When on book buying expeditions she always kept an eye out for books she thought I could use. Many that I had given up ever finding were spotted by Cynthia at some obscure book fair.

Joan Temo—a dear friend and talented artist who created the illustrations for this book.

The staff of Crofton Public Library (Crofton, MD) and the Interlibrary Loan Department of Anne Arundel Public Library System. Everyone was always ready to help the "Vampire Lady" obtain some often hard-to-find but much-needed book. These wonderful people exemplify what is right about our public libraries.

FOREWORD

It has been a hundred years since Bram Stoker published Dracula, one of the most frightening and compelling supernatural stories ever written. Indeed, his vision of an undead vampire who lives on human blood continues to haunt the darkest recesses of our collective consciousness. In the century since the appearance of Stoker's novel, the vampire legend has been kept alive and, more importantly, has been adapted to the attitudes and mores of a rapidly changing modern world by the appearance of numerous radio plays, films, books, and articles.

Historically, Dracula and other vampires had been perceived as evil, sinister figures who preyed upon innocent victims in the dark of night. Over the past several decades, however, the popular perception of vampires gradually has expanded. Much of this change has been facilitated by the publication of hundreds of books which portray vampires in a variety of non-traditional roles, including aliens from outer space, private detectives, and time travelers. In many novels, vampires are sympathetic, romantic, erotic, funny, or confused individuals who must cope with the frustrations and demands of late twentieth-century societies. For more traditional readers, there still are plenty of Dracula-like vampires who are enigmatic and terrifying.

Vampire Readings is an extremely useful bibliography for readers interested in recently published books about "old" and "new" vampires. The 779 entries in *Vampire Readings* are divided into five categories. The chapter on novels, which is by far the largest part of the bibliography with 280 entries, provides a useful guide to the many roles played by vampires, all of which are important components of western popular culture. The chapters entitled "Anthologies and Novellas" and "Young Adult" further divide the literature. The "Additional Readings" chapter enables the reader to consult more literature.

Vampire Readings thus is a welcome addition to the literature of the undead. Moreover, the author, who has had a long interest in vampires, has provided the reader with an exceptional guide to a subject that at-

tracts ever-increasing numbers of readers who are obsessed with the supernatural beings who lurk in the shadows of the night.

Thomas P. Ofcansky
Washington, D.C., and Whitby, England

INTRODUCTION

Vampire Readings is an annotated bibliography of vampire literature emphasizing fiction published since 1987 but which also includes selected older works. There are sections for novels, anthologies and novellas, young adult fiction, and additional readings. In this last area are listed nonfiction works that cover both vampire literature and myth.

For the purpose of inclusion in this book, vampires are defined as immortal (or long-lived), blood-drinking humanoids. They may go about by day and revel in sunlight, see their reflection in the mirror, laugh when confronted with a cross (or other religious object), run about without concern for native soil, savor the odor of garlic, sleep in beds and spurn coffins, but if they wish a place in this bibliography they must drink blood and be almost indestructible. I will admit that the careful reader of this tome will find a few items that push the limits of the definition, but as in life (or unlife, as the case may be), there are gray areas. When trying to draw a line of demarcation there are things that straddle the border and a judgment call has to be made.

I first encountered the vampire through a reading of Bram Stoker's *Dracula*. At the time I was staying in a guest house in Mexico City. My room had dark paneling and dim lighting—in other words, an atmosphere exactly right for what is, by even today's cynical standards, a very scary story. Many others have continued to use Count Dracula or others of his ilk to personify evil and bring shivers of fear to the reader. *Dracula* is not the first vampire story in English, but it has proven to be one of the most popular; published in 1897, *Dracula* has been continuously in print ever since. It has also spurred a spate of novels, many of which carry on the tradition of the vampire as the embodiment of evil.

In these novels of horror the supernatural powers of the undead stem from an unholy bargain, and if the vampire still has a soul, it is one that is damned. In novels such as John Steakley's *Vampire$* or *Bloodshift* by Garfield Reeves-Stevens, the undead face true death as they battle agents of the Roman Catholic Church. These agents often belong to a

1

secret group known only to certain highly placed members of the Vatican who consider vampires the spawn of Satan. Rarely do religions other than Christianity enter into the fray, although there are exceptions. In Christopher Pike's young adult series, *The Last Vampire*, Lord Krishna has a prominent role, and in *Blood of Our Children* by Matt Wartell, a Jewish holy man is one of those who must confront and conquer a vampire scourge.

Novels of the science fiction genre often offer a pseudo-scientific reason for the vampire, explaining it as the product of a mutation or a biochemical agent or as a creature of extraterrestrial origins. Examples of the last possibility can be found in *Those of Our Blood* by Jacqueline Lichtenberg and *The Madness Season* by C. S. Friedman. Works such as Wm. Mark Simmons' *One Foot in the Grave* and William Hill's *Vampire's Kiss* rely on the biochemical angle. Fantasy, on the other hand, often mixes magic with mythical demons, as in David Gemmell's *Morningstar*. Then there are the stories of Laurell K. Hamilton that have a little bit of everything. Her heroine, Anita Blake, while fending off the amorous advances of the incredibly handsome vampire Jean-Claude, contends with a variety of creatures from werewolves to zombies.

As Anita Blake, who made her reputation as a vampire slayer, reluctantly admits, certain vampires have an alluring, romantic appeal. The irresistible attraction of the vampire is a theme that has spurred many stories, several published in the romance genre. Romance writers Lori Herter, Maggie Shayne, and Nancy Gideon have written series with vampire heroes and heroines. Even writers outside this genre have used strong romantic themes as elements of their plots. In *Anno-Dracula* by Kim Newman, the love between the good vampire Geneviève and her mortal lover Beauregard gives them a combined strength that helps bring about Dracula's downfall. Count Saint-Germain, the vampire hero of Chelsea Quinn Yarbro's series, always has a romantic interest.

Where there is romance, eroticism can not be far behind. Several novels and anthologies have been created with this as a central theme. *The Kiss* by Katherine Reines and *The Darker Passions: Dracula* by Amarantha Knight are prime examples. Of course many stories and novels are a mixture of love and the erotic; Maria Kiraly's *Mina* and *Child of the Night* by Nancy Kilpatrick come to mind. Lesbian and gay themes are also explored in anthologies such as *Daughters of Darkness*, edited by Pam Keesey, as well as novels like *Diary of a Vampire* by Gary Bowen.

The terrible intimacy that the image of the vampire conjures, combined with its superior prowess and immortality, provide much raw material for a writer's imagination. They result in stories laced with mystery, adventure, romance, even humor. It is hoped that this bibliography will give readers some idea of the wide variety of stories with vampire characters or themes that are available. Something to suit everyone's taste, so to speak.

Countless vampire stories are printed every year. This book makes no pretense of being all-encompassing but should enable the reader to find titles and authors worth seeking out and to appreciate innumerable themes that can be developed around a vampire character or protagonist.

Readers are invited to contact the author via e-mail at infoseek@bibliography.com and to view the *Vampire Readings* web site at http://www.bibliography.com/vamp/

NOVELS

About annotations in this section:

For some series the annotation will cover the entire spectrum of the work and only briefly, if at all, address the content of individual titles. This is done especially in cases where all the novels should be read in order of publication so as to understand the full story that the author is trying to portray.

In instances when a film or TV series has been made based on a book, this will be noted.

If there is some characteristic to the vampire novel that is slightly off-beat, broaches other genres, or touches on a special vampiric quality, this will be noted at the end of the annotation in a field called Element(s). The following is a key to the Element(s) tags.

Bathory—Countess Elizabeth Bathory. The bloody escapades of this Hungarian noblewoman have inspired many vampire stories.

Category Romance—Love between the main protagonists is the most important element of the story. Such novels will usually be found in the romance section of bookstores or libraries.

Dracula—Pertains to either Stoker's mythical Dracula or the historical warlord Vlad Tepes (Vlad the Impaler).

History—The historical setting is an essential part of the plot.

Humor—The comic aspect is important to the story.

Mystery—A mystery is central or important to the plot. The vampire may in these cases be either the detective or the perpetrator of the crime to be solved.

Romance—A loving relationship is essential to the story but not necessarily dominant. At times a qualifier is added—such as erotic, lesbian, or gay—to give the reader a better idea of what to expect.

SF/F—Science Fiction/Fantasy. Often the SF/F elements (such as sword and sorcery, alternate history, time travel, space travel, alien vampires, or a medical explanation for vampirism) will be noted in the annotation. However there are times when the SF/F element—whatever it may be—is a surprise part of the plot. In those cases the annotation itself will give no clue. You must read the book to find what that SF/F element is.

1.   **Aldiss, Brian W.** *Dracula Unbound.* New York: HarperPaperbacks, 1991. Paperback.

In a far future when Lord Dracula and his evil minions rule, one courageous man tries to send a warning to the past. And in the world of today, another man unearths the tomb of a humanoid millions of years old. This will lead to a time-travel adventure to save mankind from the horror that awaits centuries ahead.

Element(s): SF/F, Dracula.

2.   **Andersson, C. Dean.** *I Am Dracula.* New York: Zebra, 1993. Paperback. (Revised and expanded version of *Crimson Kisses,* published by Avon in 1981 and written with Nina Romberg under the pseudonym Asa Drake.)

In this first-person narrative Vlad Dracula recounts how he became one of the most powerful of vampires. As a young man he meets and falls in love with the beautiful witch Tzigane. She tells him of a prophecy in which he will play a central role. He has been chosen to be Satan's king on Earth. Together they will rule. This certainly appeals to Dracula, but he neglects to look for the dark hidden clauses which accompany any pact with the Devil. This is an erotic interpretation of the Dracula legend.

Element(s): Romance (erotic), Dracula.

3.   **Ashley, Amanda.** *Embrace the Night.* New York: Love Spell, 1995. Paperback.

The vampire Gabriel finds his soulmate in Sara Jayne, but although she loves him deeply, she refuses to become a vampire. Years later, her soul is reincarnated as Sarah. Now she and Gabriel vow to find a way to spend eternity together; either through death or as immortals.

Element(s): Category Romance.

4.   ———. *Deeper Than the Night.* New York: Love Spell, 1996. Paperback.

Alexander Claybourne is a bestselling writer of horror tales, most often concerning vampires. The woman he loves, Kara Crawford, begins to wonder if Alex might indeed be one of the undead, especially after she reads certain passages in his current novel.

Note: This novel falls in the realm of pseudo-vampire and is mentioned here because of the other vampire titles by the author.

Element(s): Category Romance, SF/F.

5.   ———. *Sunlight, Moonlight*. New York: Love Spell, 1997. Paperback.

There are two novels in this volume, both in the genre of romantic fantasy, but it is the second story, "Moonlight," that has a vampire theme. Two thousand years ago Navarre was made into a vampire by the beautiful Shaylyn. This change did not please Navarre and he rebuffed his maker. Now in the present, Navarre has found a mortal he can love, Adrianna. Needless to say, this does not please Shaylyn.

Element(s): Category Romance.

6.   **Atkins, Peter.** *Morningstar*. New York: HarperPaperbacks, 1992. Paperback.

A serial killer called Morningstar by the police and press has maimed and disfigured his many victims. Reporter Donovan Moon gets an exclusive interview with this murderer, who justifies his actions by claiming to be a vampire hunter. The violence portrayed in this novel is quite graphic.

7.   **Aycliffe, Jonathan.** *The Lost*. New York: HarperPrism, 1996. Hardcover.

Michael Feraru returns to Romania and the ancestral lands of his grandparents. A visit to the deserted family estate, Castel (sic) Vlaicu, high in the Carpathian mountains, brings him face-to-face with the vampiric horror that haunts his bloodline. A frightening tale told through letters and diaries, much like Stoker's *Dracula*.

8.   **Bainbridge, Sharon.** *Blood and Roses*. New York: Diamond, 1993. Paperback.

In a nineteenth-century rural village, several young women become afflicted with a wasting illness, and one socially prominent debutante actually succumbs from loss of blood. William Praisegood, a London physician, arrives to investigate and concludes that a vampire is behind these villainous deeds. Dr. Praisegood's investigation also reveals that, like their human counterparts, some vampires are good and others are evil. This story is told through witty conversations reminiscent of romance/regency novels.

(*See* #322 for a short story featuring Dr. Praisegood.)

Element(s): Category Romance, Mystery.

9. **Baker, Nancy.** *The Night Inside*. New York: Fawcett Columbine, 1994. Hardcover. (Paperback, retitled *Kiss of the Vampire*, New York: Fawcett, 1995.)

In modern-day Toronto, the vampire Dimitri Rozokov, ill and weak from the long sleep of the undead, is captured by a group of gangsters specializing in snuff movies. To feed their captive, they kidnap Ardeth Alexander, a young graduate student. She soon realizes that her captors are more beastly than the crazed being who needs her blood.

Element(s): SF/F, Romance.

10. **Baker, Scott.** *Ancestral Hungers*. New York: Tor, 1996. Hardcover.

Herpetologist David Bathory knows the myths of his ancestors from the Dracul and Bathory families, but he dismisses it all as superstition. Then his life takes a sudden, bizarre turn. On a trek across country he meets Dara, whose presence causes a transformation of his being. He accumulates incredible powers and uses them to confront an unknown evil. Then he learns he is a dhampire—child of a vampire—who will become one of the undead himself some day unless his mother's Naga blood (another source of magic and power) can save him.

Element(s): Romance.

11. ———. *Dhampire*. New York: Pocket Books, 1982.

The dhampire are children of vampires. They even have certain powers over the undead. This story has been expanded and published as *Ancestral Hungers* (*see* entry #10).

12. **Beath, Warren Newton.** *Bloodletter*. New York: Tor, 1996. Paperback. (Hardcover. Tor, 1994.)

Novelist Stephen Albright is convinced that the vampiric creature of his popular Bloodletter series has come to life in the form of the serial killer Diver Dan. Beverly Hills psychologist Eva LaPorte tries to help

Stephen, who believes only his own death can stop the monster. Lots of gory dismemberment litters this tale.

13. **Bennett, Nigel, and P. N. Elrod.** *Keeper of the King.* New York: Baen, 1997. Hardcover.

Richard is a medieval knight chosen by Lady Sabra to join the ranks of the undead. These vampires serve the Goddess and have several duties, the most important of which is to protect King Arthur. Now in modern-day Toronto, Richard performs a similar function for the prime minister, who has been targeted for assassination by a cunning killer named Charon. There are several plot twists including a quest for the Holy Grail and a race to save Lady Sabra from a terrible fate.

Note: Nigel Bennett, as fans of the TV series *Forever Knight* will know, played the vampire La Croix. Bennett's face, in his vampire guise, is prominently displayed on the book jacket.

Element(s): SF/F, Romance.

14. **Bergstrom, Elaine (aka Marie Kiraly).** Austra Family series.

Besides being wealthy artisans, the Austras are an ancient family of vampires. They are aliens who resemble humans but definitely are not, nor ever were, members of the human race. These vampires drink human blood but can also subsist on that of animals. Additionally they have at their disposal a special, secret formula that allows them to survive without sanguinary substance for long periods. Several family members are introduced throughout the four novels that currently comprise the series. The Austra character who appears in each novel is the handsome, magnetic Stephen. Because various family members are introduced in each novel, reading the books in order of publication will provide the reader with a greater appreciation of this epic story.

15. ———. *Shattered Glass.* New York: Jove, 1989. Paperback. (Paperback. New York: Ace, 1994.)

Series: Austra Family No. 1.

In 1955 Stephen Austra goes to Cleveland to renovate the stained glass windows of St. John's Cathedral. He falls in love with Helen, a neighbor and artist who also happens to have inherited some Austra blood from a grandfather. Charles, Stephen's dark twin, also lurks about, looking for a way to die and end his personal anguish. In the meantime, Charles causes many grisly deaths.

Element(s): Romance, SF/F.

16. ———. *Blood Alone*. New York: Jove, 1990. Paperback. (Paperback. New York: Ace, 1994.)
   Series: Austra Family No. 2.
   The story begins in the years just prior to World War II. The Austra family business is headquartered in Portugal and managed by Stephen. He hires a new employee, Paul Stoddard, a mortal who becomes a trusted friend. Because of their wealth and extensive holdings throughout Europe, the Austras become targets of Nazi spies and saboteurs. The love life of Stephen's nephew Laurence and Paul's own strong feelings for an Austra woman play important roles in this complex tale.
   Element(s): Romance, SF/F.

17. ———. *Blood Rites*. New York: Jove, 1991. Paperback. (Paperback. New York: Ace, 1994.)
   Series: Austra Family No. 3.
   Helen and Stephen marry and move to an isolated area of the Canadian wilderness. Here their sons, Patrick and Dickie, are born. But danger arrives when the mob tracks Helen's uncle, Richard Wells, to their home. In the line of duty Richard had killed the son of a mobster kingpin. Helen, still uneasy with her transformation, must quickly come to terms with the vampiric powers of her Austra heritage.
   Element(s): Romance, SF/F.

18. ———. *Daughter of the Night*. New York: Jove, 1992. Paperback. (Paperback. New York: Ace, 1994.)
   Series: Austra Family No. 4.
   Sixteenth-century Europe saw much cruelty, but even for those times Elizabeth Bathory stood out as unusually sadistic. In this story Elizabeth finds a kindred spirit in the Austra family rebel and outcast, Catherine. Elizabeth not only revels in blood and torture but also seeks the kind of immortality reserved for beings like her friend Catherine. Stephen (called Steffen in this book) along with several other members of the family, plays a prominent role in the denouement.
   Element(s): Bathory, Romance, SF/F.

19. **Billson, Anne.** *Suckers*. New York: Atheneum, 1993. Hardcover.
   Set in contemporary London, this darkly comic novel is narrated by the sardonic Dora, who suddenly finds herself surrounded by a horde of hungry, yuppie vampires.
   Element(s): Humor.

20. **Bischoff, David.** *Nightworld.* New York: Ballantine, 1979. Paperback.

On a planet named Styx, a Victorian-like society is ruled by Satan, whose fearsome creatures, including the dreaded vampires, prey on the human population. But Oliver and Geoffrey discover that Satan is actually Hedley Nicholas, a cyborg psychotic who made these monsters from metal and living tissue and programmed them to obey his evil instructions.

Element(s): SF/F.

21. ————. *Vampires of Nightworld.* New York: Ballantine, 1981. Paperback.

Satan is dead but his creatures, now on their own, are even more terrifying. Knowing the vampires to be the most menacing of the monsters, Oliver sets himself the task of destroying them. This job becomes even more perilous when he comes up against the ruthlessly ambitious vampire Vlad Paler.

Element(s): SF/F.

22. **Black, Campbell.** *The Wanting.* New York: McGraw-Hill, 1986. Hardcover.

In the small town of Carnarvon, near San Francisco, a strange wasting illness strikes children and sometimes adults. Louise and Max have moved here with their son Dennis. A charming elderly couple befriend the boy. Then he begins to show signs of illness.

Note: The vampiric element here is mainly energy draining, but the "vampires" also sup on human blood.

23. **Bowen, Gary.** *Diary of a Vampire.* New York: Rhinoceros (Masquerade Books), 1995. Paperback.

The setting is 1990's Baltimore. In the hope of restoring the will to continue his unlife, Rafael Guitierrez puts himself into a long sleep. The plan was for him to sleep four years; instead, he sleeps fifteen and is only awakened when his nephew, Michael, breaks into the house, setting off the alarm. Rafael's lover, James, had promised to maintain the house and guard his investments, but James betrayed that trust. In his despair, Rafael turns for comfort to Michael. This novel contains much graphic sex along with some S & M.

Element(s): Romance (gay, erotic).

24. **Brand, Rebecca (aka Suzy McKee Charnas).** *The Ruby Tear.* New York: Forge (Tom Doherty), 1997. Hardcover.

A family curse hangs over the Griffins and the enormity of it falls on the eldest son of each generation. The last of the Griffins is the wealthy playwright Nicolas, who decides to confront the enemy that has haunted his family for centuries, by writing a play which in certain ways parallels his family's battle with this demon. The enemy is Ivo von Cragga, a man who became a vampire when he made a pact with the Blood Angel, a creature that inhabits the violence-charged Balkans. An ancestor of Nicolas had betrayed Ivo's family, murdered them, and stolen the Ruby. Ivo has exacted revenge on every generation. Now Nicholas is the target, and the vampire decides to strike by first attacking the woman Nicholas loves: Jessamyn Croft, who has the lead part in his play. Ivo's strategy, however, runs into trouble when he too comes to love Jessamyn.

Element(s): Romance.

25. **Briery, Traci, and Mara McCuniff.** *The Vampire Memoirs.* New York: Zebra, 1991. Paperback.

Series: The Vampire Memoirs No. 1.

Mara, a young woman of fourth-century Britain, had a loving husband, Gaar, and three children. However, Agyar, the first vampire, transforms her into one of his kind and tears her from her family. He wants her for his bride, but she cannot forget or forgive Agyar's murder of Gaar. Mara runs away but cannot escape her monstrous vampire nature. It is almost 1600 years before she can finally get her revenge.

Note: the narrator of this story is Mara McCuniff. She is also, according to the title page, a co-author. Even the copyright is in the names of Briery and McCuniff. So maybe these really are vampire memoirs.

Element(s): Romance.

26. **Briery, Traci.** *The Vampire Journals.* New York: Zebra, 1993. Paperback.

Series: The Vampire Memoirs No. 2.

Theresa has been a vampire for 200 years, and was transformed by the centuries-old Agyar, the same being who changed Mara. Unlike Mara, Theresa loves being one of the undead, and she resents the way Mara depicted her in *The Vampire Memoirs*. Now she tells her side of the story.

Element(s): Romance.

27. **Brite, Poppy Z.** *Lost Souls*. New York: Dell, 1993. Paperback.
    (Hardcover. New York: Delacorte, 1992.)
    In the dark, sensual world of the vampire, a child named Nothing comes of age and learns the pleasures and curses that come with his heritage. He finds Zillah, the seductive vampire who fathered him on a young groupie mortal woman. The reality of his and his father's nature is quite brutal. A complex, sometimes gory, scenario plays out in the underworld of New Orleans, Louisiana, and Missing Mile, North Carolina.

28. **Brondos, Sharon.** *Kiss of Darkness*. New York: Silhouette, 1994.
    Paperback.
    Publisher Series: Silhouette Shadows #32.
    Master Death orders his vampire servant Adrian Smith to kill scientist Sue Cooper, a beautiful woman who may have found a way to extend human life for decades. But Adrian falls in love with Sue, and together they must find a way to outwit Death and save themselves.
    Element(s): Category Romance, SF/F.

29. **Brust, Steven.** *Agyar*. New York: Tor, 1993. Hardcover.
    The word "vampire" is never mentioned in this riveting story, but through the journal of Jack Agyar the reader comes to understand that he is indeed one of the undead. Agyar has been summoned to a small town in northeastern Ohio by his maker, Laura. In the course of his stay he meets two mortals, Jill and Susan. His interaction with them brings profound changes to all their lives.
    Element(s): Romance.

30. **Butler, Jack.** *Nightshade*. New York: Atlantic Monthly Press, 1989. Hardcover.
    John Shade owns a ranch on a Martian colony. John's vampirism is a secret, but someone finds out and uses that as leverage to recruit him in a war against a growing rebellion. John narrates the story and gives some interesting background on vampirism. For instance, all vampires he has known ended their human existence in an especially horrible way. He theorizes that there is in certain humans a kind of latent, ultimate survival mechanism that causes the transformation.
    Element(s): SF/F.

31. **Byers, Richard Lee.** *Netherworld*. New York: HarperPrism, 1995.
    Paperback.

Publisher series: World of Darkness: Vampire.

Close to dusk, on a stretch of beach near a Tampa Bay pier, Zane finds the mutilated body of his girlfriend, Rose. When he returns a few moments later with a cop, the body is gone; only her shredded clothes remain. No trace of blood can be found. No one believes Zane until a chance encounter with Sartak, an 800-year-old Mongol vampire who agrees to help because he loves a good mystery. This page-turner has lots of fast-paced action.

Element(s): Mystery.

32. **Cadnum, Michael.** *The Judas Glass.* New York: Carroll & Graf, 1996. Hardcover.

Richard pricks his finger on an antique mirror which had mysteriously arrived one day at his house. Not long after this incident he dies and is buried. Nine months later, he awakens in his coffin as a vampire. Now as he comes to terms with his new unlife he also uses his vampiric powers to find the killer of his lover Rebecca. And he realizes that, if he can awaken as one of the undead, it may be possible for Rebecca as well. This is a poetic telling of a human life transformed.

Element(s): Romance.

33. **Caine, Geoffrey.** *Curse of the Vampire.* New York: Diamond, 1991. Paperback.

Abe Stroud is a former Chicago police detective as well as an archaeologist and anthropologist. This training and his psychic abilities come in handy when a series of bizarre deaths occur in a small Illinois town. With the help of coroner Martin Magaffey, Abe unearths an entire community of undead.

Element(s): Mystery, SF/F.

34. **Cartier, Annee.** *Redemption.* New York: Pinnacle, 1997. Paperback

In Victorian England, actress Gabriela Rozina performs in plays at the famous Drury Lane Theater. This theater is also the secret hiding place of vampire Marcus Danewell. Although he vowed never again to love a mortal female, he finds himself strongly drawn to Gabriela. When he finally reveals himself to her, she too is attracted to him. Still, he tries to discourage her by showing her the hellish life led by one of the undead. She loves him nonetheless.

Element(s): Category Romance.

35. **Charnas, Suzy McKee (aka Rebecca Brand).** *The Vampire Tapestry*. New York: Simon & Schuster, 1980. Hardcover. (Trade paperback published by Living Batch Press, Albuquerque, NM, 1993.)

Edward Weyland is a popular professor of anthropology and a vampire who secretly feeds on those whose trust he has gained. He prides himself on his predatory skills and his superiority to mortals. But perhaps there is a streak of humanity in his tormented soul after all: Edward begins to feel a certain empathy with his prey. This is a truly unique twist on the vampire theme and a skillful look at a vampire's psychological profile.

36. **Ciencin, Scott.** Danielle Walthers series.

Samantha Walthers adopts an abandoned baby girl and names her Danielle. When Danielle reaches adulthood, she meets a group of vampires who inform her that she is an Initiate, the child of a vampire father and human mother. (Only male vampires can reproduce.) Danielle's new friends, and in particular the handsome Bill Yoshino, want to bring her into the vampire world—a ritual that includes sex, an exchange of blood, and the killing of a human by Danielle. Samantha discovers her daughter's vampiric background and vows to save her soul. The journey this portends and the horrors encountered make up the trilogy. The vampires in Ciencin's world consist of Ancients, who have the greatest powers, and their various generational offspring. The first of their race was a Roman Centurian, present at the Crucifixion, who drank some of Jesus' blood.

37. ———. *The Vampire Odyssey*. New York: Zebra, 1992. Paperback.
Series: Danielle Walthers No. 1.

Danielle meets the vampires who tell her she can be one of them, but only when she shares their blood and then kills and drinks the blood of a mortal. Meanwhile Samantha, knowing that her daughter's soul is in danger, frantically searches for her.

38. ———. *The Wildings*. New York: Zebra, 1992. Paperback.
Series: Danielle Walthers No. 2.

Danielle has turned her back on the vampires, but before escaping their clutches, she had gone through part of the transformation—thus giving her some vampiric powers. Among those powers is that of healing and she want to use this to help people. Unfortunately, other vampires still abound and they are after Danielle.

39. ———. *Parliament of Blood*. New York: Zebra, 1992. Paperback. Series: Danielle Walthers No. 3.

Danielle and Samantha are in hiding, but a powerful vampire finds them. Danielle is offered a terrible bargain. From here the plot becomes very complex, but always fast-paced.

40. **Collins, Nancy A.** *Midnight Blue: The Sonja Blue Collection*. Stone Mountain, GA: White Wolf, 1995. Paperback.

This is a trilogy. (In this edition the three novels are bound together.)

Sonja Blue is a vampire and a vampire killer. Filled with rage for what she has become, she seeks the one who caused her transformation. With her new vampiric awareness, Sonja sees the Real World, a place which is inhabited by Pretenders—preternatural creatures, most of them horrifying, like ogres, incubi, succubi, ghouls, werewolves and, of course, vampires. But there are also the seraphim, angelic creatures with powers that frighten the others. To ordinary mortals, without the gift of second sight, the Pretenders appear human. In this trilogy Sonja's powers grow swiftly as she learns about her true nature and follows every possible clue that will lead her to Morgan, the vampire father she wants to destroy. Sonja must also battle a part of herself that she dubs the Other, a demonic part that continually threatens to destroy what humanity she has left.

41. ———. *Sunglasses after Dark*. Stone Mountain, GA: White Wolf, 1995.

In *Midnight Blue: The Sonja Blue Collection*.

Sonja finds a scholar who though human knows about and has an understanding of the Pretenders. He also explains to her that he believes her to be a powerful vampire like no other.

42. ———. *In the Blood*. Stone Mountain, GA: White Wolf, 1995. In *Midnight Blue: The Sonja Blue Collection*.

Private Investigator William Palmer is hired by the vampire Dr. Pangloss to find Sonja. Pangloss knows that Sonja's power is the only thing that will stop the terrible experiments of Lord Morgan—the man who also happens to be Sonja's maker.

43. ———. *Paint It Black*. Stone Mountain, GA: White Wolf, 1995.
    In *Midnight Blue: The Sonja Blue Collection*.
    Sonja's anger and powers increase and fuel the supercharged end-
ing to this trilogy.

44. ———. *A Dozen Black Roses*. Clarkston, GA: White Wolf, 1996.
    Hardcover.
    Publisher series: World of Darkness: Vampire.
    In this novel Sonja Blue enters White Wolf's World of Darkness.
She is a vampire like no other that the Kindred of Deadtown have ever
come across. Sinjon of the Ventrue clan holds control of Deadtown until Esher, a member of the Tremere, challenges his authority and makes
a bid for control. Sonja, known throughout this novel as the stranger,
has her own agenda. She still hates vampires and has no compunction
about destroying them. In Deadtown she meets a five-year-old boy
whose beautiful mother has been kidnapped by Esher. Sonja promises
the child that she will get his mother back. She has a plan that means
playing one powerful Kindred chief off against the other. The story takes
place after the events in *Paint It Black* (*see* #43).

45. **Collins, Toni.** *Something Old*. New York: Silhouette, 1993. Pa-
    perback.
    Publisher series: Silhouette #941.
    Gabby Thorne is a descendent of the Van Dammes, an old, dis-
tinguished family of vampire hunters. Still, when she finally falls in love,
the object of her affection, Adrian Lacross, just happens to be one of the
undead.
    Element(s): Category Romance.

46. **Cooke, John Peyton.** *Out for Blood*. New York: Avon, 1991. Pa-
    perback.
    The doctors tell Chris Callaway that they may be able to keep his
leukemia in remission for another five years. But Beth has a better offer.
She's willing to give Chris immortality as a vampire. Chris accepts, then
learns that staying "alive" as a vampire has its own problems. One problem is a vampire hunter who keeps himself eternally youthful by bathing
in the blood of vampires.

47. **Courtney, Vincent.** *Vampire Beat*. New York: Pinnacle, 1991.
    Paperback.

Series: Christopher Blaze No. 1.

Christopher Blaze is a Miami police detective who infiltrates and helps destroy the Cannus cult, a group responsible for many deaths. Before he dies in a hail of bullets, their leader, Batiste Legendre, puts a curse on Chris, saying that he will become one of the undead. It seems Batiste had some real influence. Not long after this incident Chris himself is shot, dies, and turns into a vampire. The first thing he does is volunteer for the graveyard shift, since now he can only work at night. His new powers give him some advantages, but there are also problems. The biggest of these concerns the other vampire in the city, the evil, 300-year-old Yosekaat Rakz.

Element(s): Mystery.

48. **Cresswell, Jasmine.** *Prince of the Night.* New York: Topaz, 1995.

Dakon, Count of Albion, is one of a race who call themselves Vam-pyr. To procreate, the males perform a vigorous, lusty mating with human females while sucking their blood. When Dakon finally takes a young woman to his bed, she does not survive the encounter. Dakon is devastated and vows never to again touch a woman. Then he meets Cordelia Hope and falls in love.

Element(s): Category Romance, SF/F.

49. **Cusick, Richie Tankersley.** *Buffy the Vampire Slayer.* New York: Pocket Books, 1992. Paperback.

Airhead and high school cheerleader Buffy wants nothing more than to "graduate from high school, go to Europe, marry Christian Slater, and die." But the mysterious Merrick tells her she is one of the chosen who have the ability to kill vampires and save humanity. She reluctantly sets about the task of staking the undead.

Note: This is a novelization based on the 1992 movie *Buffy the Vampire Slayer,* which has also been made into a TV series.

Element(s): Humor.

50. **Daniels, Les.** Don Sebastian series.

In this gothic-style series, Don Sebastian de Villanueva, Spanish nobleman, wizard, and vampire, rises—literally—into turbulent periods of history. In these stories he often seems to die at the conclusion only to be resurrected years later by another, less powerful, wizard or alchemist. Although not a creature of pure evil, Sebastian is quite capable of cruelty. His crimes, however, pale in comparison to those of the mortals around him.

51. ————. *The Black Castle*. New York: Scribner's, 1978. Hard-cover. (Paperback. New York: Ace, 1979.)
Series: Don Sebastian No. 1.
This story takes place during Spain's infamous Inquisition. Don Sebastian inhabits the family castle, which most people believe is aban-doned. He is writing a book on witchcraft for his brother, the local Grand Inquisitor. This brother keeps his vampire sibling "alive" by al-lowing him access to Inquisition victims. The brothers hate one an-other, but, for the time being, each needs the other.
Element(s): History.

52. ————. *The Silver Skull*. New York: Scribner's, 1979. Hardcover. (Paperback. New York: Ace, 1983.)
Series: Don Sebastian No. 2.
In the New World, Cortez has invaded the land of the Aztecs and battles them for control of Tenochtitlan. Don Sebastian, with the help of a beautiful Aztec priestess, becomes the god Smoking Mirror, and uses his powers to help the native people fight against the conquistadors.
Element(s): History.

53. ————. *Citizen Vampire*. New York: Scribner's, 1981. Hard-cover. (Paperback. New York: Ace, 1985.)
Series: Don Sebastian No. 3.
Don Sebastian is resurrected during the French Revolution. His benefactor is a beautiful countess who is soon caught by the mob and condemned to death. The Countess's maid, Madeleine, becomes a bloodthirsty member of the rabble and calls for death to the aristocracy. Readers are treated to introductions of famous figures such as Robes-pierre, the Marquis de Sade, and Dr. Guillotine.
Element(s): History.

54. ————. *Yellow Fog*. West Kingston, RI: Donald M. Grant, 1986. Illustrated by Frank Villano. Hardcover. (Paperback. Revised edition. New York: Tor, 1991.)
Series: Don Sebastian No. 4.
Don Sebastian reappears in mid-nineteenth century England. He becomes enamored of the lovely, wealthy Felicia, who longs to become

his disciple. Her ne'er-do-well fiancé, Reginald, sees what is happening and tries to stop their liaison. The consequences of such impertinence are terrible indeed.

Element(s): History.

55.   ———. *No Blood Spilled*. New York: Tor, 1991. Paperback.
Series: Don Sebastian No. 5.

This title is a sequel to *Yellow Fog*, at the end of which Don Sebastian has himself boxed and shipped to Calcutta. His plan is to contact the remnants of the disbanded, murderous group known as Thugs. This band specializes in killing by strangulation with a scarf because their goddess Kali forbids them to spill blood. Sebastian's next goal is to make contact with the dreadful Kali herself. He feels they have much in common. Meanwhile, Reginald Callender, whose fiancée was stolen away by Sebastian in *Yellow Fog*, has escaped from a lunatic asylum and pursues Sebastian to India, vowing to put a stake through his heart.

Element(s): History.

56.   **Darke, David (aka Ron Dee)**. *Shade*. New York: Zebra, 1994.

Scarlett Shade is a popular writer of vampire fiction. Her fans are legion and completely enveloped in the world created by her stories. Some fans become so mesmerized by her words that they commit suicide, hoping to be resurrected as one of the undead. It comes as no surprise to one reader, Phillip Ottoman, that Scarlett is a vampire. He has the bites to prove it. Of course, everyone else thinks he is crazy. Scarlett's novels and the author herself appeal to the erotic side of life. Sex and death are what she writes about and what enchant her fans.

57.   **Davis, Jay, and Don Davis**. *Bring on the Night*. New York: Tor, 1993. Paperback.

A vampire and a vampire slayer are each on a killing spree in modern-day Chicago. Homicide Detective Dennis Coglin must stop both. The vampire Nathan Kane takes special delight in psychologically tormenting his victims before taking his sanguinary pleasure.

Element(s): Mystery.

58.   **Dee, Ron (aka David Darke)**. *Blood*. New York: Pocket Books, 1993. Paperback.

Dr. Miller is conducting secret experiments with terminally ill patients. These patients miraculously recover, but with troubling side effects like tremendous, uncontrollable urges for sex and blood. Trish Blaine and Fred Langston of the Life Center, where Miller is employed, are asked to investigate his work. They discover that he has unleashed a virus that can have terrifying consequences for humanity.

Element(s): SF/F.

59. ———. *Blood Lust*. New York: Dell, 1990. Paperback.

The Rev. Ben Dixon teams up with another minister, Warren MacDonald, to fight a master vampire who has recently moved to St. Louis. There the ministers are joined by Emily Knox, whose parents have been transformed into vampires. Alongside the spiritual motivation of the protagonists are scenes of graphic sexual violence.

60. ———. *Dusk*. New York: Dell, 1991. Paperback.

Walt, a U.S. Immigration officer, has disappeared; he was last seen near a Texas ghost town on the U.S.–Mexican border. Another agent, Samantha, who is also Walt's lover, stays overnight in this deadly town hoping to find out what happened to him. She finds Walt, but he has changed. He is a vampire, and he promises her that she can join him and others like him. In fact, he insists on it. She decides to fight for her humanity instead.

61. **Devine, Thea.** *Sinful Secrets*. New York: Zebra, 1996. Paperback.

Declan Sinclair has been asked to discreetly find the whereabouts of Queen Victoria's trusted secretary, Mr. Luddington. While searching in a small town, Declan is kidnapped. Meanwhile a young, voluptuous woman, Sayra Mansour, who works as a position girl (a Victorian-era stripper) is also kidnapped. Both end up as captives of the decadent begoun of Kabir, who takes great delight in watching Declan and Sayra having sex—lots of it. These two finally manage to escape but not before discovering the begoun and Luddington sucking blood from slave girls. Declan and Sayra make their way to London, all the while pursued by a fiend named Ferenc. They then discover that the vampire influence is wider than they thought.

Element(s): Romance (erotic).

62. **Dillard, J. M.** *Bloodthirst*. New York: Pocket Books, 1987. Paperback.

Publisher series: Star Trek #37.

Disaster strikes Federation outpost Tanis. Two bodies are found, one of which is almost completely drained of blood. A survivor is severely anemic, sensitive to light, and terribly gaunt. It doesn't take a rocket scientist to figure out what his problem is. However, discovering the cause behind this mayhem is a little trickier.

Element(s): SF/F.

63. **Dvorkin, David.** *Insatiable.* New York: Pinnacle, 1993. Paperback.

Richard Venneman has a natural animal magnetism that makes him irresistible to many women and not a few men. Richard, however, does not find sex all that interesting until he encounters Elizabeth, who shows him how delightful it can be. Of course he does not realize she is a vampire until he wakes up the next night in a funeral parlor with a terrible thirst for blood. More surprises are in store for Richard as he tries to figure out what to do about the abomination he has become.

64. **Eccarius, J. G.** *The Last Days of Christ the Vampire.* San Diego: III Publishing, 1988. Paperback.

This novel takes a bizarre approach to the vampire myth. In a small town, Professor Holback learns of a Christian cult whose members say that Christ appears to them. Holback has a theory for what is happening. He feels the story of Jesus is a metaphor for the vampire, but when he tells others about these thoughts, he finds the metaphor to be reality. As the title indicates, the tone of this novel is very anti-Christian.

Element(s): Religion.

65. **Elrod, P. N.** The Vampire Files series.

Jack Fleming is the protagonist of this series, which takes place largely in 1930s gangster-ridden Chicago. He became a vampire through his love affair with Maureen. Although most humans are immune to the vampire bite, those who are not transform at death. Jack finds out in the first book—*Bloodlist*—that he will survive as one of these ageless, eternal creatures. Jack is befriended by the mortal Charles Escott, a private investigator, who helps him in his various adventures. As a vampire Jack casts no reflection in a mirror, can dematerialize, needs a bit of dirt from home, and, of course, has a thirst for human blood. The writing style throughout is fast-paced, witty, even ironic.

66. ———. *Bloodlist.* New York: Ace, 1990. Paperback.
Series: The Vampire Files No. 1.

Jack wakes up dead. Someone has murdered him. Now he needs to find out who before that person has a chance to do it again. Charles aids him in this effort.

Element(s): Mystery, Romance.

67. ———. *Lifeblood*. New York: Ace, 1990. Paperback.
Series: The Vampire Files No. 2.
Jack finds himself pursued by an amateurish vampire hunter. Although this would-be Van Helsing is no real threat, another more sinister and savvy hunter appears. Jack searches for his former lover, Maureen, and eventually meets her sister, now an old woman.

Element(s): Mystery, Romance.

68. ———. *Bloodcircle*. New York: Ace, 1990. Paperback.
Series: The Vampire Files No. 3.
Jack desperately misses Maureen and will not rest until he finds out what has happened to her. With Charles at his side, he follows clues that lead him to Maureen's former lover, Jonathan Barrett (*see* Jonathan Barrett series #72–76). After a couple of murders and attempted murders, the mystery of Maureen is finally solved.

Element(s): Mystery, Romance.

69. ———. *Art in the Blood*. New York: Ace, 1991. Paperback.
Series: The Vampire Files No. 4.
Jack becomes a friend to a group of young artists. When one of them is brutally murdered, he uses his special vampiric powers to track down the killer.

Element(s): Mystery, Romance.

70. ———. *Fire in the Blood*. New York: Ace, 1991. Paperback.
Series: The Vampire Files No. 5.
Jack and Charles take on what seems to be a straightforward case. A diamond bracelet has been stolen, and the wealthy Sebastian Pierce wants the private eyes to recover it, quietly, with no police involvement. The prime suspect is Stan McAlister, a small-time hood who is a friend of Marian Pierce, daughter of Sebastian. Jack sets out to find Stan and question him. Unfortunately, by the time Jack locates the right apartment, Stan is dead—murdered, in fact. Now things really become complicated.

Element(s): Mystery.

71. ———. *Blood on the Water*. New York: Ace, 1992. Paperback.
Series: Vampire Files No. 6.
Jack has made an enemy of gangster Vaughn Kyler, a man so formidable that Jack's powers to probe mortal minds have absolutely no effect on him. Kyler wants Jack truly dead. Jack's situation is not helped when he encounters Angela Paco, daughter of the man who murdered Jack in *Bloodlist* (*see* #66) and brought him into his undead state. In this novel our hero comes close to meeting his final end in the murky waters of Lake Michigan.
Element(s): Mystery, Romance.

72. ———. Jonathan Barrett, Gentleman Vampire series.
Jonathan is a young American living during the time of the rebellion against England. His wealthy, loyalist family consists of a loving father and a sister, Elizabeth, to whom Jonathan is very close. His mother is a nasty woman whose vile nature makes everyone miserable. Jonathan and Elizabeth do whatever possible to keep out of her way. This series depicts life for the upper classes in England and the American colonies.

73. ———. *Red Death*. New York: Ace, 1993. Paperback.
Series: Jonathan Barrett, Gentleman Vampire No. 1.
While studying in England, Jonathan becomes enamored of Nora Jones, a vampire. They exchange blood, but Nora does not tell Jonathan what might happen to him, and he is much too young and innocent to figure it out. Jonathan returns home, where he is killed in a skirmish between rebels and Hessian soldiers near his home. He awakens as a vampire.
Element(s): History, Romance.

74. ———. *Death and the Maiden*. Ace, 1994. Paperback.
Series: Jonathan Barrett, Gentleman Vampire No. 2.
Jonathan tries to contact Nora through his English cousin Oliver, but no one has seen her in months. Meanwhile, Elizabeth falls in love with and marries Lord James Norwood, a man who turns out to be something other than he seems.
Element(s): History, Romance.

75. ———. *Death Masque*. New York: Ace, 1995. Paperback.
Series: Jonathan Barrett, Gentleman Vampire No. 3.

After a brief return to America, Jonathan and Elizabeth once more journey to England, where Jonathan hopes to find out what has happened to Nora. They stay with cousin Oliver and must deal with Oliver's trouble-making mother. Then there is the seductive, distant cousin, Clarinda, who puts all of them in danger.

Element(s): History, Mystery, Romance.

76. ———. *Dance of Death*. New York: Ace, 1996. Paperback.
Series: Jonathan Barrett, Gentleman Vampire No. 4.

Jonathan discovers that he has a son, a four-year-old born from an earlier indiscretion. He has a wonderful reunion with his child, but Clarinda is still causing problems. She is willing to do anything to get what she wants, even put the child in danger. The good news is that Jonathan at last finds Nora.

Element(s): History, Mystery, Romance.

77. ———. *I, Strahd*. Lake Geneva, WI: TSR, 1993. Hardcover.
Publisher series: Ravenloft.

A human inhabitant of the mist-shrouded land of Barovia braves the poisonous air that surrounds Castle Ravenloft, home of the evil ruler and vampire Lord Strahd. Here, the human finds a diary in which Strahd has set down his life as mortal warlord and the incident that precipitated his Faustian pact with Death. He thought he would have his heart's desire: life with the lovely Tatyana. Instead, he is condemned to eternal psychic torment.

Element(s): Romance (dark).

78. **Elvira, and John Paragon.** *Elvira: Transylvania 90210.* New York: Boulevard, 1996. Paperback.

Lots of tongue-in-cheek, low-grade humor permeates this story as camp vamp queen Elvira helps Beaver Hills High School student Luke Berry find his missing girl friend, Shannon Doheny. It seems that a gorgeous hunk named Sevil Alucard (read the name backwards) has recently moved into the neighborhood. But Elvira knows there is something not quite right about this guy. She is right. He is a vampire, and he now has Shannon sharing his coffin.

Note for non-TV viewers: This story is a parody of the evening soap *Beverly Hills 90210*.

Element(s): Humor.

79. **Erickson, Lynn.** *Out of the Darkness.* New York: Harlequin, 1995. Paperback.
    Publisher series: Harlequin Superromance #626.
    Miguel Rivera y Aguilar, a handsome Spaniard born 500 years ago, meets Karen, a night nurse in New York City, and falls in love. He confides in her the torment he suffers because of the creature he has become. He is driven by one desire—to kill Baltazar, his nemesis and the monster who turned Miguel into a vampire.
    Element(s): Category Romance.

80. **Farren, Mick.** *The Time of Feasting.* New York: Tor, 1996. Hardcover.
    Modern-day vampires have learned to survive on nourishment from blood banks, but every seven years or so their predatory nature flares out of control. Renquist, Master of the New York enclave, will allow the hunt only under controlled circumstances, but his leadership is being openly challenged by a group of younger members. Adding to his problems are the determined efforts of two knowledgeable vampire hunters. This is a literate look at the vampire life.

81. **Fenn, Lionel.** *The Mark of the Moderately Vicious Vampire.* New York: Ace, 1992. Paperback.
    Series: Kent Montana.
    On a dark and stormy night a purple dinghy crashes ashore, discharging a coffin and its occupant on the rocky shores of Assyria, Maine. The vampire Count Lamar de la von Zaguar is looking for a deserted manor in which to set up housekeeping, hunt for food and maybe find a bride to spend eternity with. Unfortunately for him, Kent Montana—Scottish baron, sometime actor, and part-time inhabitant of Assyria—has arrived, summoned by a mysterious message telling of dire events in this small town. With the help of some of the eccentric folks (like the pert and pretty Roxy) who populate Assyria, Kent figures out just what sort of creature the town's newest citizen must be.
    Element(s): Humor, Romance.

82. **Flanders, Eric.** *Night Blood.* New York: Zebra, 1993. Paperback.
    Val Romero is a vampire with a conscience. He drinks and kills to satisfy an overpowering hunger for blood, but he tries to choose his victims carefully and to take only those who menace human society. Sometimes, however, he makes mistakes. One of these mistakes brings the un-

wanted attention of a federal investigator as well as some vampire hunters with their own agenda. In an unusual twist, the question of what happens to a vampire's freed soul is explored.

83. **Ford, John M.** *The Dragon Waiting: A Masque of History*. New York: Simon and Schuster, 1983. Hardcover. (Paperback. New York: Avon, 1985.)

In this alternate history-cum-fantasy, vampirism is a dread disease, and most of those afflicted hide their condition. The time is roughly that of the early Renaissance. Five people, one a vampire, meet at an inn and, with a wizard as their leader, join forces to help the English Plantagenet King Edward IV and his brother, who will in time become Richard III. Vampirism plays an interesting role in the fate of Richard's nephews.

Element(s): SF/F.

84. **Foster, Prudence.** *Blood Legacy*. New York: Pocket Books, 1989. Paperback.

At Castle Csejthe, where the notorious Elizabeth Bathory spent her last days, an old tomb is accidentally opened. Months later, Ferencz Nadasday of Csejthe arrives in a small Florida town to find and awaken the reincarnated spirit of Elizabeth, which resides in the body of bookstore owner Angelique Gaudet. Father Ponikenus, a priest who knows about vampires, and police Lieutenant Gil Spencer, Angelique's lover, help her in the fight to save her soul.

Element(s): Bathory, Romance.

85. **Friedman, C. S.** *The Madness Season*. New York: DAW, 1990. Paperback.

The Earth and many other worlds have been conquered by the Tyr, a terrible race which commands subservience, inspires fear, and does not tolerate diversity. One of those who fought in earth's war against the conquerors is Daetrin, a man who has lived for centuries. Through the course of this complex novel Daetrin must come to grips with the alien part of himself—a part that among other things craves blood—before he can do what is necessary to free earth and the other inhabited worlds of their oppressors.

Element(s): SF/F.

86. **Gemmell, David.** *Morningstar*. New York: Del Rey, 1993. Paperback.

This sword-and-sorcery adventure takes place in a world much like that of medieval Scotland, but one in which magic and demons have reality. The narrator is Owen Odell, a bard and magicker, who tells how an amoral thief named Jarek Mace becomes the famed warrior hero Morningstar, a man who leads a vanquished people against their oppressors. Two hundred years ago this land had been conquered by the Angostins. Fighting against this human army is not much of a problem for Morningstar and his band of rebels, but when the evil Vampire Kings of legend return and take control of the conquering army Jarek faces a foe that makes even a hero quake.

Note: The vampires in this story live on blood, but it must be from a person who has some goodness within. The blood of someone purely evil is useless.

Element(s): SF/F.

87. **Gerrold, David.**

In Gerrold's two-book series there is a great deal of adventure in both novels, which really constitute one story.

Eons ago, humans genetically engineered a supremely aggressive race called the Phaestor to protect them from the Predator, a deadly enemy sweeping the galaxy. The Phaestor are vampires living on blood and terror. After doing the job for which they were created, the Phaestor declare themselves the master race. To help carry out their deadly rule they use terrifying sentient creatures called Moktar Dragons—another genetically engineered life form but this one modeled on that nasty predatory dinosaur known as the velociraptor. On a forbidding planet in a tiny cluster outside the Milky Way, an assortment of humans and their allies are beginning to assert themselves by launching a rebellion against the vampire oppressors. There are many twists and turns to the plot, and the characters do not always act as expected.

Note: Based on "Trackers," created by Daron J. Thomas and David Gerrold.

88. ———. *Under the Eye of God.* New York: Bantam, 1993. Paperback.

The fascinating cast of characters that propel the plot are introduced. In a cliffhanger ending some humans find themselves at the not-so-tender mercies of Phaestor leader Lady Zillabar.

Element(s): SF/F.

89. ———. *Covenant of Justice*. New York: Bantam, 1994. Paperback.
The humans and their allies finally get their act together and the rebellion takes form.
Element(s): SF/F.

90. **Gideon, John.** *Kindred*. New York: Jove, 1996. Paperback.
In the 1970s, Lewis Kindred was in Vietnam, where the horrors of war paled in comparison to the vampire creature he encountered: one that tortured, killed, and fed on blood and anger. That creature wanted to bring Lewis into its world, but Lewis refused. Now, more than twenty years later, the creature once again seeks him out, manifesting itself in a bloody killing spree.

91. **Gideon, Nancy.** *Midnight Kiss*. New York: Pinnacle, 1994. Paperback.
Book one in a trilogy.
Arabella Howland is the daughter of a physician who has a patient with an intriguing ailment—a penchant for human blood and an aversion to sunlight. The patient, Louis Radman, is a vampire, and Dr. Howland feels he has found a cure. Indeed Louis' condition seems to revert for a while. He indulges his love for Arabella and they marry. But their happiness is marred by the arrival of Bianca Du Maurier and Gerardo Pasquale, vampires from Louis' past. It is safe to say these two do not have Louis' best interests in mind. Bianca, for instance, wants to see her former lover return to his vampire status. And, in this novel, that is a distinct possibility.
Element(s): Category Romance.

92. ———. *Midnight Temptation*. New York: Pinnacle, 1994. Paperback.
Book two in a trilogy.
Louis and Arabella have a teenage daughter, Nicole. One night she follows her father and watches as he feeds on the blood of a young woman. Horrified that her father is a monster, she runs away to make a new life for herself in Paris. There she meets and falls in love with Marchand LaValois, but their happiness is soon marred by the appearance of the vengeful Bianca and her companion Gerardo.
Element(s): Category Romance.

93. ———. *Midnight Surrender*. New York: Pinnacle, 1995. Paperback.

Book three in a trilogy.

Manhattan is now home to Louis and Arabella. Louis still appears young and virile, but Arabella has refused the dark kiss of the vampire. Now she is an elderly woman. Although her husband is completely devoted to her, Arabella knows that at eighty her time is limited. She feels Louis needs another with whom he can share his life. She decides Cassie Alexander is perfect for the role. Cassie is young, independent, lovely, and in desperate need of help. Someone is stalking her and murder is on that person's mind.

Element(s): Category Romance, Mystery.

94. **Golden, Christie.** *Vampire of the Mists*. Lake Geneva, WI: TSR, 1991. Paperback.

Publisher series: Ravenloft.

This novel is the first in TSR's Ravenloft dark fantasy series. A golden elf named Jander Sunstar has been one of the undead for five centuries. He had led an unhappy existence until he met Anna, a beautiful woman who did not shun him. But she suffered and eventually died because of a terrible magic that emanated from the land of Barovia. Jander is transported there and must confront the evil magician and fellow vampire Count Strahd Von Zarovich.

(*See* #77 for a novel about Strahd.)

Element(s): Romance, SF/F.

95. **Golden, Christopher.** *Of Saints and Shadows*. New York: Jove, 1994. Paperback.

Within the Vatican is a book called *The Gospel of the Shadows*. It holds secrets about a group most believe does not exist—vampires. When this book disappears Liam Mulkerrin, a priest and magician with a penchant for murder, sets out to retrieve it. Also in pursuit is Peter Octavian. He is a vampire, but an unusual one in that he does not kill. Peter eventually discovers many of the secrets about his race that are written in the Gospel. He also learns that the Church plans to annihilate all vampires in one bloody conflagration.

Element(s): Religion.

96. ——. *Angel Souls and Devil Hearts*. New York: Berkley, 1995. Paperback.

This sequel to *Of Saints and Shadows* takes place five years later. Vampires, who prefer the term Shadows, know a freedom unheard of in the history of their existence. They become part of the human world and abide by its laws. But this peaceful coexistence is threatened. First, there are the vampires who despise this accommodation. In their view, vampires should be feared. They should prey on humans. Then there is Liam Mulkerrin, whose magic powers have increased. He plans to use these powers in his insane dream to reshape the world.

97. **Gomez, Jewelle.** *The Gilda Stories*. Ithaca, New York: Firebrand Books, 1991. Paperback.
   Gilda's life as a vampire begins in Louisiana, shortly before the Civil War. She is a young runaway slave found by a white female vampire who hides her and grooms her to become the replacement in the life of the vampire's lover, Bird. This vampire, also named Gilda, has grown weary and seeks true death. Thus begins the saga of an African-American, lesbian vampire as she seeks goodness and meaning in an often hostile world. This novel spans the period of 1850 to the not-so-distant future of 2050.
   Element(s): History, Romance (lesbian).

98. **Gottlieb, Sherry.** *Love Bite*. New York: Warner, 1994. Paperback.
   Rusty is a vampire who has lost the love of her life, Gregor. He was also a vampire, but he recently met true death. Now Rusty is looking for someone to love. While doing so, she leaves more than a few blood-drained male bodies. Los Angeles homicide detective Jace Levy reluctantly concludes that a vampire is behind the killings. He also finds himself attracted to Rusty. The feeling is mutual.
   Element(s): Mystery, Romance.

99. **Griffith, Kathryn Meyer.** *The Last Vampire*. New York: Zebra, 1992. Paperback.
   In an apocalyptic future the earth is wracked by earthquakes, a plague sweeps the planet, and nuclear bombing becomes commonplace. Emma barely survives this holocaust. She is badly burned by radiation, but a chance encounter with a vampire saves her. Now she is a vampire and must have blood to live. Later she meets Matthew, a mortal, and falls in love. A time comes when she may have to forfeit her existence to save his.
   Element(s): Romance, SF/F.

100. **Grimson, Todd.** *Stainless*. New York: HarperPrism, 1996. Paperback.

There is a dreamy, poetic feel to this love story between the vampire Justine and a mortal, Keith. Justine has been undead for a long time, but her memories are fragmented and difficult for her to retain. She rarely kills, but when she does, Keith disposes of the bodies. A somber mood pervades this novel. Life and unlife have many difficulties. For Justine and Keith the reawakening of a vampire accidentally created by Justine brings about a traumatic climax.

Element(s): Romance (dark).

101. **Haley, Wendy.**
The following two novels should be read as one story.

One member of Savannah's ultra-rich Danilov family is happy to welcome distant cousin Alex from Europe. Margaret, now eighty years old, knows he is a vampire born almost 1,000 years ago. However, two centuries earlier he had a mortal wife and children. The Danilovs are the descendents of this marriage. When Margaret dies, Barron, who had assumed he would be heir, promises to break Alex, who inherited almost everything. This does not worry our vampire hero, but he is concerned about the seductive charms of two Danilov women, Lydia and Sonya, both of whom bring his Blood Hunger to fever pitch. Adding to his problems is the evil Suldris whose terrible empire Alex destroyed some 400 years ago. Suldris finds an unwitting ally in Lydia, whose desperate hunger for Alex leads her into a pact with this cruel mage. The repercussions from this terrible bond carry through both novels.

There are two bright spots in Alex's life. The first is Elizabeth, a woman who knows his nature yet has no fear of him. Instead she wholeheartedly gives Alex her love. The second is Justin, the teenage son of Sonya and Barron and a young man desperately in need of fatherly love and acceptance. Alex happily fills that role. Good character development makes these romanticized vampire novels worth reading.

102. ———. *This Dark Paradise.* New York: Diamond, 1994. Paperback.

Alex takes over the Danilov family empire which earns him the enmity of his "cousin" Barron who had aspired to run things. To make things worse for Alex, his ancient enemy Suldris has tracked him down. There is some happiness for Alex, however. He meets and falls in love with Elizabeth.

Element(s): Category Romance.

103. ———. *These Fallen Angels*. New York: Diamond, 1995. Paperback.

The luscious Lydia has gained some magical powers from Suldris. Now she uses them in an attempt to destroy Alex and Elizabeth. This will be her revenge for Alex's rejection of her.

Element(s): Category Romance.

104. **Hambly, Barbara.** *Those Who Hunt the Night*. New York: Del Rey, 1988. Hardcover.

Someone has been killing the vampires of London, and Oxford professor James Asher is forced into investigating this "crime" by the long-undead Simon Ysidro. Aiding Asher's efforts is his physician wife, Lydia. This is an engrossing mystery set in Edwardian England.

Element(s): Mystery, SF/F.

105. ———. *Traveling with the Dead*. New York: Del Rey (Ballantine), 1995. Hardcover.

In this sequel to *Those Who Hunt the Night*, James Asher sights a vampire he recognizes speaking conspiratorially with a known Austrian spy. Asher decides to follow them when they depart England. The chase leads across Europe all the way to Constantinople. Lydia enlists the aid of Simon Ysidro when she realizes that her husband has gotten himself into a desperate situation.

Element(s): Mystery, SF/F.

106. **Hamilton, Laurell K.** Anita Blake Vampire Hunter series.

All manner of things that go bump in the night inhabit modern-day America, and in particular the city of St. Louis. There are zombies, ghouls, shapeshifters, and vampires. The undead have been accorded constitutional rights. Anita Blake, who made her reputation as a vampire slayer, now toils as an animator, raising the dead in the form of zombies. She is also attached to a new police unit called the Regional Preternatural Investigation Team, commonly referred to as the Spook Squad. In order to follow the developing relationships among Anita, the vampire Jean-Claude, and the werewolf Richard, it is best to read the books in order of publication.

107. ———. *Guilty Pleasures*. New York: Ace, 1993. Paperback.

Series: Anita Blake Vampire Hunter No. 1.

Anita's reputation for stalking blood-drinking immortals has come to the attention of vampire master Nikolaos. She believes Anita is the perfect sleuth to find out who has been murdering local vampires. Anita agrees to undertake this mission because the life of her good friend Catherine will be terminated by Nikolaos if she does not comply. Although Anita professes an aversion to all vampires, she finds herself reluctantly attracted to Nikolaos' rival for master of the city, the incredibly handsome Jean-Claude. The feeling is definitely mutual.

Element(s): Mystery, Romance.

108. ———. *The Laughing Corpse*. New York: Ace, 1994. Paperback.
Series: Anita Blake Vampire Hunter No. 2.

This story has more to do with zombies than vampires. A killer zombie has been raised by a powerful animator, and the police ask Anita's help in tracking down this beast and putting it to rest. They also want to apprehend the person who animated the monster. A vampire presence is supplied by the sexy master Jean-Claude, who helps Anita with the investigation.

Element(s): Mystery, Romance.

109. ———. *Circus of the Damned*. New York: Ace, 1995. Paperback.
Series: Anita Blake Vampire Hunter No. 3.

Vampires are a contentious lot. A rogue master vampire and his followers have been killing mortals and leaving their victims in plain view. Once again, Anita's help is sought by the police. She agrees to help, but this master is old and powerful and wants to use Anita to destroy master of the city Jean-Claude. Readers are also introduced to Richard, a werewolf, who becomes a love interest for Anita.

Element(s): Mystery, Romance.

110. ———. *The Lunatic Cafe*. New York: Ace, 1996. Paperback.
Series: Anita Blake Vampire Hunter No. 4.

Things heat up between Richard and Anita. There is even talk of marriage, but Jean-Claude wants equal time with Anita and promises not to kill Richard if she will date him as well. Meanwhile, werewolves are disappearing at an alarming rate. Are they being killed or kidnapped? Anita has a devilish time finding out.

Element(s): Mystery, Romance.

111. ———. *Bloody Bones*. New York: Ace, 1996. Paperback.
Series: Anita Blake Vampire Hunter No. 5.

The mutilated bodies of three teenage boys have been found in the Ozark mountains. Anita believes this to be the work of a rogue vampire, but she is unsure. This is a difficult case, and she needs the help of someone with special knowledge of the undead to help her solve it. So she swallows her pride and calls upon Jean-Claude. In the course of this story, Anita comes to terms with her feeling for this extraordinarily handsome immortal, although she is still in love with Richard.

Element(s): Mystery, Romance.

112. ———. *The Killing Dance*. New York: Ace, June 1997. Paperback.

Series: Anita Blake Vampire Hunter No. 6.

Sabin, a vampire, and his human servant, Dominic, come to Anita for help. Sabin's body is ravaged by a horrible rotting disease, and he and Dominic believe that Anita may be able to help with a magic spell. Anita's magical powers have increased in a way that surprises even her. She promises to try. Meanwhile someone has put out a high-priced contract on Anita's life. In the midst of this, Richard must confront a moral dilemma. He wants to lead the local werewolf pack, but he wants to do it without killing anyone, including the current leader, Marcus. Anita's feelings for Richard and Jean-Claude intensify. The complex relationship that these three share is the primary focus of this novel.

Element(s): Mystery, Romance.

113. **Harbaugh, Karen.** *The Vampire Viscount*. New York: Signet, 1995. Paperback.

Publisher series: Signet Regency Romance.

Nicholas St. Vire, rich, desirable and handsome, has a dark secret. He is a vampire who desperately wants to restore his humanity. He hopes that an arranged marriage to the lovely, unsuspecting Leonore Farleigh will provide the special ingredient he needs to make the transformation.

Element(s): Category Romance.

114. **Harrison, Jane.** *Dark Dreams*. New York: Zebra, 1996. Paperback.

The Grigori are the spawn of the fallen angels who followed Lucifer in his rebellion against heaven. They use their dark powers against humans, but a few seek salvation and peace with Heaven. This story centers on one such angel who lives as a mortal in Memphis,

Tennessee, in 1865. He falls in love with Lucy Bry. Meanwhile a plague of insects settles over Memphis, and vampires—created by other dark angels—roam the city. The love between Lucy and Victor, with the aid of a priest named Michael (the Archangel in disguise), provides the means to save the people of the city from certain destruction.

Element(s): Category Romance, SF/F.

115. **Hauf, Michele.** *Dark Rapture.* New York: Zebra, January 1997. Paperback.

Sebastian DelaCourte, vampire and rock singer, is deeply attracted to the lovely Scarlet Rose. Scarlet gives in to Sebastian's dark kiss, becoming one of the undead. But they still must contend with a spirit's possession of Scarlet and the dangerous enmity of Francesco, a vampire and former friend of Sebastian. Their friendship ended when Sebastian accidentally killed a lady loved by Francesco.

Element(s): Category Romance.

116. **Herber, Keith.** *Dark Prince.* New York: HarperPrism, 1994. Paperback.

Publisher series: The World of Darkness: Vampire. (This is the same series published by White Wolf.)

In modern-day San Francisco, 150-year-old vampire Sulliven is ordered by The Grandfather, an elder, to dispose of another member of the Kindred. This brings Sulliven into the escalating war among the city's clans. He barely escapes destruction. This novel displays a shadowy world where vampires glory in the seamier side of "life"—drug trafficking, prostitution, S & M—all the nasty things which both attract and repel us.

117. **Herbert, Brian, and Marie Landis.** *Blood on the Sun.* New York: HarperPrism, 1996. Paperback.

Publisher series: The World of Darkness: Vampire. (This is the same series published by White Wolf.)

The story begins in Seattle, Washington, 1942, while America is in the midst of WW II. This is a war of mortals and not something of interest to most Kindred. But Desidra is an exception. She angers her superior, Prince Romano, when she insists it would be in the Kindred's interest to help the war effort. He banishes her from his group. Now on her own, Desidra decides to follow her conscience. One of her first acts of patriotism is to warn the U.S. Pacific Fleet about Admiral Yamamoto's plans to crush it at Midway.

Element(s): History.

118. **Herter, Lori.**

Lori Herter's quartet of vampire novels centers on the lovely, mortal Veronica and the handsome vampire David de Morrissey, a playwright who once studied under William Shakespeare. The setting is contemporary, and, although the locales vary, much of the action takes place in Chicago, where David and Veronica reside.

119. ———. *Obsession*. New York: Berkley, 1991. Paperback.

David and Veronica meet and fall desperately in love. But David feels Veronica has not seen enough of life to commit to a vampire existence with him. He insists on a ten-year separation, to which she reluctantly agrees. The reader also meets Darienne Victoire, a vampire friend and former lover of David. Unlike our hero, Darienne loves all that the vampire life has to offer.

Element(s): Category Romance.

120. ———. *Possession*. New York: Berkley, 1992. Paperback.

During the separation from Veronica, David begins an affair with violin maker Alexandra Peters. The romance sours when she insists that he turn her into a vampire. Meanwhile Darienne has fallen in love with Matthew McDowall, a mortal actor who stars in one of David's plays. Veronica, although always in David's thoughts, makes no real appearance in this novel.

Element(s): Category Romance.

121. ———. *Confession*. New York: Berkley, 1992. Paperback.

Veronica believes she has found something that can cure David's vampirism. He is skeptical but willing to try. The romance between Darienne and Matthew does not progress smoothly. In fact, he feels repulsed when he learns of her true nature.

Element(s): Category Romance.

122. ———. *Eternity*. New York: Berkley, 1993. Paperback.

David is cured but fears he is returning to the vampiric state. Matthew finally accepts Darienne's condition. All the lovers live happily ever after.

Element(s): Category Romance.

123. **Hill, William.** *Dawn of the Vampire.* New York: Pinnacle, 1991.
    Paperback.

South Holston Lake, bordering Tennessee and Virginia, holds dark secrets. An old town and cemetery lie beneath its waters. When two divers decide to explore the site, one ends up with his throat torn out and all blood drained from his body. The other becomes possessed by Viktor Von Damme, a vampire who has discovered the secret of walking in daylight. Now that he is free he plans to release others like himself from their watery graves. But Von Damme has a rival vampire group to contend with as well as the tenacity of Troy Bane, a reporter who gathers a group of friends to help him find an answer to the nightmare that has engulfed the area.

124. ———. *Vampire's Kiss.* New York: Pinnacle, 1994. Paperback.

David, a popular writer of horror fiction, lives as a recluse because of a rare blood disease, porphyria. His skin is pale and his eyes reddened. An evil and beautiful vampire, Monique, tells him he has begun the "transformation." David fights his attraction to her and turns to his minister for help. The power of religious beliefs is treated respectfully in this novel.

Element(s): Religion.

125. **Holland, Tom.** *Lord of the Dead: The Secret History of Byron.*
    New York: Pocket Books, 1996. Hardcover.

The noted poet Lord Byron recounts to a frightened young woman the harrowing events that led to his becoming a vampire of tremendous power, a true Lord of the Dead. While traveling through nineteenth-century Greece, he was befriended by a centuries-old Turk who lured him into the vampire life and then seemingly murdered the one woman Byron had ever loved, the beautiful slave Haidée.

Elements: Romance.

126. **Huff, Tanya.** Vicki Nelson series.

Vicki Nelson is a former Toronto homicide detective turned private investigator. She left the police force because of a deteriorating eye disease, retinitis pigmentosa. In a series of adventures—all with supernatural or science fiction elements—she teams up with former lover and Toronto police detective Mike Carlucci as well as the vampire and romance novelist Henry Fitzroy, illegitimate son of England's King Henry VIII. Tension develops between Henry and Mike since both love Vicki. In most of these adventures the men find themselves reluctant allies.

127. ———. *Blood Price*. Daw: New York, 1991. Paperback
     Series: Vicki Nelson No. 1.
     A young man who has suffered taunts from others decides to gain power through a pact with a blood-hungry demon whom he conjured up. The demon goes on a terrifying killing spree. Fast action abounds as Vicki, Mike, and Henry track down and destroy the killer.
     Element(s): Mystery, Romance, SF/F.

128. ———. *Blood Trail*. New York: Daw, 1992. Paperback.
     Series: Vicki Nelson No. 2
     Set in farm country near London, Ontario. A family of werewolves is being systematically murdered. The survivors ask their friend Henry Fitzroy for help. He, in turn, calls upon Vicki's investigative talents to ferret out the killer. Mike also shows up to help.
     Element(s): Mystery, Romance, SF/F.

129. ———. *Blood Lines*. New York: Daw, 1993. Paperback
     Series: Vicki Nelson No. 3.
     Henry is having nightmares about the sun. These horrifying dreams are caused, it turns out, by a paranormal link to another powerful lifeforce. An Egyptian mummy, buried and bound with ancient spells, has been awakened. It becomes Henry's task, aided by Vicki and Mike, to stop the evil plotted by this creature and his god.
     Element(s): Mystery, Romance, SF/F.

130. ———. *Blood Pact*. New York: Daw, 1993. Paperback.
     Series: Vicki Nelson No. 4.
     Both Mike and Henry openly admit their love for Vicki. They are, as usual, antagonists and allies. With some difficulty they put differences aside when Vicki's mother dies suddenly. Guilt consumes Vicki because she had not returned repeated calls from her mother. Her distress is compounded when Mrs. Nelson's body disappears. Her mother had worked at the Queen's University Life Science Department for Dr. Aline Burke. Vicki and her two friends uncover Dr. Burke's ghastly secret experiments to reanimate the dead. For the breakthrough step in

the experiment, a fresh body was needed. How convenient that Mrs. Marjory Nelson had a heart condition.

Element(s): Mystery, Romance, SF/F.

131. ———. *Blood Debt*. New York: Daw, 1997. Paperback.
    Series: Vicki Nelson No. 5.

One sunset, when Henry awakens from his vampiric sleep, he finds the apparition of a young man at the foot of his bed. The ghost does not speak but still manages to communicate the desire to avenge his murder. Henry, now residing in Vancouver, calls on Vicki to help in this investigation. He is desperate to find answers because the ghost has shown a power to kill when frustrated in its efforts. Vicki agrees to make the cross-country trek, and Mike insists on going with her. Not long after the apparition first appears, the naked body of a young man is fished from Vancouver Harbor. He has recently had a kidney surgically removed. Some criminal group is apparently trafficking in body parts.

Element(s): Mystery, Romance, SF/F.

132. **Jac, Cheryln.** *Night's Immortal Kiss*. New York: Pinnacle, 1992. Paperback.

In a desperate search for her missing brother, former police detective Rachel Domecq enters the old mansion where the reclusive Beaumondier family resides. They are an ancient family of vampires, but she does not realize this until after she falls in love with the handsome Alexandre. There are some interesting twists in this romantic tale.

Element(s): Category Romance, Mystery.

133. ———. *Night's Immortal Touch*. New York: Pinnacle, 1995. Paperback.
    This is a sequel to *Night's Immortal Kiss*.

Alexandre's sister, Suzanne, survived the fire that destroyed her ancestral home and all of the Beaumondier family except her brother. Now a year later, more trouble enters her life. A vampire killer is on the loose in New Orleans and Suzanne is a suspect. Meanwhile, she finds herself attracted to homicide detective Clay Garnier, who returns her affection.

Element(s): Category Romance, Mystery.

134. **Johnson, Oliver.** *The Forging of the Shadows*. New York: Roc, 1997. Paperback.

Series: The Lightbringer Trilogy. Book one.

This is a sword-and-sorcery epic with a world facing doom and a prophecy that promises hope. The sun is dying and the forces of darkness, the worshippers of Iss, God of Death, have grown strong. The city of Thrull suffers the most. Seven years ago Lord Faron Gaton and his vampire hordes took over. Now mortals trapped within Thrull hide in their homes at night. To satisfy the prophecy and search for artifacts of power, three followers of Reh, God of Light, set out on their quest. Urthred is a priest of Reh and knows magic, Jayal is a young nobleman whose father once ruled Thrall, and Thalassa is a woman loved by Jayal but now used as a plaything of Lord Gaton. Magic and evil fiends make their adventures more than a little harrowing.

Element(s): SF/F.

135. **Kalogridis, Jeanne.** The Diaries of the Family Dracul series.

The descendents of Vlad Tsepesh (Dracula) have a covenant with this most famous nosferatu, and, in this trilogy, the horror of what that covenant implies manifests itself. The story begins in 1845 with the death of Arkady Tsepesh's father in Transylvania. Heartbroken, Arkady returns for the funeral along with his pregnant wife, Mary. Arkady assumes his father's position as manager of his great-uncle's estate. Although he has always revered, even loved, his Uncle Vlad, Arkady slowly realizes that a monster lurks in Dracula's soul, and that his own soul and that of his newborn son may soon be forfeit. The trilogy takes place over a span of fifty years and brings the reader up to the time of Stoker's novel. The story plays out as Arkady and others like Bram Van Helsing seek to destroy the evil that is Dracula. This is not an easy task because the Prince of Darkness has powerful allies, one of them being the vampiress Elizabeth Bathory, a creature even more brutal than he.

Like Stoker, Kalogridis tells her tale through a series of journal and diary entries by the various characters. The denouement gives an unusual twist to the Dracula story and the nature of the vampire. (The final volume, *Lord of the Vampires,* has an interesting forward by noted expert Dr. Elizabeth Miller, professor of English at Memorial University of Newfoundland.)

136. ———. *Covenant with the Vampire.* New York: Delacorte, 1994. Hardcover.

Series: The Diaries of the Family Dracul No. 1.

Arkady and his pregnant wife, Mary, return to the family's ancestral

home. Only gradually does the horror of his uncle's true nature and the terrible covenant imposed on the family become known to Arkady. In desperation he plans to escape with his wife and newborn son.
Element(s): Dracula.

137. ————. *Children of the Vampire*. New York: Delacorte, 1995. Hardcover.
Series: The Diaries of the Family Dracul No. 2.
Arkady vows to destroy Vlad, but it may be too late. His son Stefan, now an adult, has been abducted and returned to Dracula's evil clutches. One of those enlisted to help save Stefan is Dr. Abraham Van Helsing.
Element(s): Dracula.

138. ————. *Lord of the Vampires*. New York: Delacorte, 1996. Hardcover.
Series: The Diaries of the Family Dracul No. 3.
Although this final installment in the trilogy parallels Stoker's *Dracula*, it tells a far more complex story. Van Helsing continues his pursuit of Dracula, who has suddenly acquired new strength and can leave the confines of his Transylvanian castle. Elizabeth Bathory, also an immortal, has helped Vlad in his mission, but she has her own agenda.
Element(s): Dracula, Bathory.

139. **Kells, Sabine.** *A Deeper Hunger*. New York: Leisure, 1994. Paperback.
Callie has experienced nightmares which have so consumed her that she becomes withdrawn and depressed. But within the terrible dreams there is one bright spark. For a few moments she feels herself with a man she truly loves and one who returns that love. In a desperate attempt to escape her depression, she takes her savings and goes to the beautiful, lush Hawaiian island of Maui. There she meets the man of her dreams. He is a vampire.
Element(s): Category Romance.

140. **Kelly, Ronald.** *Blood Kin*. New York: Zebra, 1996. Paperback.
Josiah Craven died in 1898 and was buried in an unmarked grave with a stake through his heart. Almost one hundred years later his great-grandson Dudley accidentally unearths the coffin and sets the vampire free to begin his reign of terror. The setting is rural Tennessee.

141. **Kilpatrick, Nancy.** *Child of the Night*. London: Raven, 1996. Paperback.

In this sensuous story of love, Carol Robins enters the vampire world one night in Bordeaux, France. She is accosted by the immortal André on an empty street where moments earlier she had seen him drink blood from the neck of a frail, elderly man. Thinking he means to kill her she bargains with her body and offers herself to him for two weeks. Intrigued and excited by her, André agrees. What neither expected was that Carol would conceive a child. André's vampire friends, an eclectic, rather interesting lot, insist that Carol have the child and leave it with them. Secretly Carol promises herself to do everything possible to escape their clutches. Throughout this novel Carol and André suffer a love/hate relationship that for the sake of their child must be resolved.

Element(s): Romance.

142. ———. *Near Death*. New York: Pocket Books, 1994. Paperback.

David Lyle Hardwick, a vampire with the sensitivity of a poet and a respect for human life, awakens one evening to find a young woman bending over him ready to pound a stake into his heart. He stops her easily. Her name is Kathleen, but her street name is Zero. She is a hooker, an addict, and one terrified lady. Someone had sent her from New York City to Manchester, England, to commit this outrageous deed. Now David needs to find out who and why. He keeps Kathleen prisoner until she is drug-free, then takes her back to New York in an attempt to solve this multi-layered mystery. A bond develops between these two as they work together. Although from very different eras and cultures, they fall in love. For Kathleen, whose life has been one of deprivation and abuse, David is like a gift from the gods.

Element(s): Mystery, Romance.

143. **King, Stephen.** *'Salem's Lot*. Garden City, New York: Doubleday, 1975. Hardcover. (There have been several reprints.)

Jerusalem's Lot, Maine, is a small town where nothing much happens. Ben Mears had spent a short time there as a child. But one nightmare from those days still haunts him. On a dare he paid a visit to the old, deserted Marsten House and came face-to-face with an apparition from hell. Now an adult, he returns hoping to exorcise the nightmares that have never left him. Instead, he slowly comes to realize that this house is a beacon for evil. A child disappears, others die mysterious deaths, and it is discovered that someone unknown, unseen and undead has moved into Marsten House. Only Ben and a young boy, Mark Petrie, have the knowledge, belief, and courage needed to battle the nosferatu. This is a classic vampire tale with lots of creepy scenes and a terrifying atmosphere that builds and builds. Not for the faint of heart!

Note: A made-for-TV movie, 1979.

144. **Kiraly, Marie (aka Elaine Bergstrom).** *Mina.* New York: Berkley, 1994.

Dracula's dark kiss awakened a passion in Mina only hinted at in Stoker's novel. This story explores the erotic feelings that consume the new Mrs. Harker. It leads her on a search for the lover who may have survived Van Helsing's stake.

Element(s): Dracula, Romance.

145. **Knight, Amarantha.** *The Darker Passions: Dracula.* New York: Masquerade, 1993. Paperback.

This is an erotic retelling of Stoker's *Dracula*. Here Vlad Tepes is the human warlord-turned-vampire who entices with his sensual and sadomasochistic charm. There is just enough plot to string together detailed scenes of passion-laced S & M. Knight's version carries the dark atmosphere of the original and has its own poetic cadence.

Element(s): Romance (erotic).

146. **Kurtinski, Pyotyr.** *Thirst.* New York: Leisure, 1995. Paperback.

The immensely wealthy William Van Diemen, a vampire who feeds and kills without pity, lives in a spectacular home overlooking the Hudson River. Van Diemen has, in his estimation, a good life, but things begin to go wrong for him when a mysterious cartel decides it wants his land and will stop at nothing to get it.

147. **Lackey, Mercedes.** *Children of the Night.* New York: Tor, 1990. Paperback.

Series: Diana Tregarde Investigation

Diana Tregarde is a powerful witch. She needs to use all her special powers to track down and defeat monstrous soul-eaters haunting the streets of New York. Fortunately, she has the help of a handsome Frenchman who also happens to be a vampire.

Element(s): Mystery, Romance, SF/F.

148. **Laymon, Richard.** *The Stake.* New York: St. Martin's, 1991.
Hardcover. (Paperback. New York: Zebra, 1995.)

Larry, a writer of horror stories, goes on an outing with some friends to an old, deserted town in the desert. While exploring the ghost town's hotel, they come across a hidden room with a mummified corpse in an open coffin. It is the body of a woman with a stake through her heart. Alternately horrified and fascinated, Larry feels compelled to remove the stake and allow the vampire to awaken.

149. **Lee, Earl.** *Drakulya.* Tucson, AZ: Sharp Press, 1994. Paperback
and hardcover.

In this literate retelling of the Dracula story, the Prince of Darkness is Mircea Drakulya, elder brother of Vlad and Radu. He has taken his brother Vlad's identity because of his fearsome reputation as the Impaler. The terror this engenders offers protection from the superstitious local peasants. Dr. Van Helsing knows vampires exist and hunts them in order to learn the secrets of eternal life. He is particularly interested in a certain Wallachian noble. Much of the story is told from Drakulya's point of view, but the tale is supplemented with letters and diary entries of Van Helsing, Jonathan Harker, Mina and others. This novel holds some neat psychological twists.

Element(s): Dracula.

150. **Lee, Tanith.** Blood Opera Sequence series.
These novels should be read in order of publication.

The Scarabae are an ancient family of vampires who live like much of the rest of humanity, but differ in that their lives can extend for centuries, and they have an occasional need for human blood. The three novels of this series center on Rachaela and her daughters Ruth and Anna. From the time she was a child, Rachaela's mother had warned her to stay away from her father's family—the Scarabae. They were evil, she had said. But the pull of the family is irresistible. Rachaela tries to hide, but they find her, and she goes to live with them in the family mansion. Here, she becomes pregnant with her first Scarabae child, Ruth. Some twelve years later, Rachaela has a love affair which produces another Scarabae daughter, Anna. Although each girl has a different father, in many ways they are chillingly the same. The Scarabae world holds many secrets, including a history that reaches back to biblical times. Tanith Lee's lyrical writing style adds to the surreal quality of this offbeat vampire saga.

151. ———. *Dark Dance*. New York: Dell, 1992. Hardcover.
   Series: Blood Opera Sequence No. 1.
   Rachaela enters the house of the Scarabae. There she meets the man who fathers her daughter Ruth. The full force of the family curse is visited on this child.
   Element(s): SF/F.

152. ———. *Personal Darkness*. New York: Dell, 1993. Hardcover.
   Series: Blood Opera Sequence No. 2.
   The Scarabae realize that Ruth has a great deal of darkness within her. They call upon another branch of the family to send someone who might be able to save her. Meanwhile Rachaela has a new lover—another Scarabae. She is once again pregnant.
   Element(s): SF/F.

153. ———. *Darkness, I*. New York: St. Martin's, 1996. Hardcover.
   Series: Blood Opera Sequence No. 3.
   Children throughout the world are being kidnapped. One who is a target of this plot is Anna, Rachaela's very precocious second daughter. In this third book the reader is given an interesting glimpse at the strange and complex history of the Scarabae family.
   Element(s): SF/F.

154. ———. *Sabella or The Blood Stone*. New York: Daw, 1980. Paperback.
   Sabella Quey lives on the colonized planet of Novo Mars. Sabella shuns the sunlight and feasts on the blood of the young men who flock around her. She teaches herself to take only enough without killing and feels guilty about those who died before she learned this lesson. Sabella believes no one knows her secret. She is wrong. Her deceased mother's sister, Cassie, knew, and in her will condemns her niece for being a creature of evil. Before her death, Cassie had set in motion a plan to destroy Sabella. But Sabella is a survivor and she has some unforeseen help.
   Element(s): Romance, SF/F.

155. **Lichtenberg, Jacqueline.** *Those of My Blood*. New York: St. Martin's, 1988. Hardcover.
   The luren, a race of vampires, live secretly among the human inhabitants of earth. One group of them, the Tourists, longs to return to their home planet while another group, the Residents, considers earth

home and have respect for human life. When an alien spacecraft crashes on the moon, these opposing factions suspect that it has come from their home world.

Element(s): Romance, SF/F.

156. ———. *Dreamspy*. New York: St. Martin's, 1989. Hardcover.

This sequel to *Those of My Blood* takes place in the area of space where the luren home world is located. A galactic war is in progress. A major point of the conflict centers on a method of faster-than-light travel that is destroying the fabric of space. Although a luren is one of the more important characters, vampires or vampirism has little to do with the plot.

Element(s): SF/F.

157. **Longstreet, Roxanne.**

The following two novels make up one story and should be read in order.

Michael Bowman, a successful surgeon in Dallas, is married to Maggie, a police detective. A friend of his, coroner Adam Radburn, is a vampire, but keeps this fact secret until one night his hypnotic guard slips and Michael notices his friend has no reflection. From this moment of realization Michael's life plunges into a nightmare existence. He tries to extricate the image of Adam's vampire essence but cannot. He confronts his friend, and, in the ensuing fight, Adam gets a taste of Michael's blood. This makes it possible for Adam to transform Michael a few days later when he dies in an automobile accident. As a vampire Michael has increased powers but he is also the target of William, a psychopathic nosferatu who takes fiendish delight in torturing and killing anyone who means anything to Adam. That now includes Michael and by extension Maggie.

158. ———. *The Undead*. New York: Zebra, 1993. Paperback.

The battle to survive William's murderous assault begins.

159. ———. *Cold Kiss*. New York: Zebra, 1990. Paperback.

The struggle continues but is complicated by the presence of the Society, a vampire group which offers their help. It too hates William, but, even so, Adam has reason not to trust its members completely.

160. **Lumley, Brian.** Necroscope series.

This series centers on the character of Harry Keogh, a necroscope, someone who has the ability to communicate with the dead through a kind of mental telepathy. The dead of Lumley's universe exist on a plane where they have consciousness but no sight or hearing. Harry's unique abilities enable him to give them a sort of window on the world again. He not only communicates with them but also makes friends with them. Some of the more brilliant, such as mathematician August Möbius, give him access to other dimensions and universes.

Harry is a member of a special branch of British intelligence known as E-Branch. Others in this branch have differing types of psychic abilities, but none as extraordinary as Harry's. Harry's main nemesis is his Russian counterpart Boris Dragosani, an evil necromancer, who wrenches secrets from the dead by torturing their corpses, even consuming body parts.

So where do vampires come in? It turns out that Dragosani has an ally, a 500-year-old Wallachian warlord and vampire by the name of Thibor Ferenczy. As the series unfolds the role of the vampire becomes more and more prominent. Vampirism spreads not through biting but when the vampire entity implants itself within the human host. Eventually the vampire takes over, destroying most remnants of the host's humanity.

The vampires originated in a parallel world. At one point Harry Keogh's son, Harry Jr., is transported to that world, where vampire lords, Wamphyri, wage war with one another when not massacring the local human populace. The place is known as Sunside/Starside.

There are several plot complications as vampirism (and other hideous evils) threatens to engulf humanity. Lumley's universe is a dark one—no levity found here—although the action and writing are fast-paced. This series, begun in 1986, has a definite cold war mentality—the Russians are usually on the side of evil.

161. ———. *Necroscope*. New York: Tor, 1986. Paperback.
   Series: Necroscope No. 1.
Harry communicates with and learns from the dead. This ability and the vast knowledge he has gained makes him a perfect operative for the British E (for ESP)-Branch. Evil is represented by Soviet agent Boris Dragosani, who is under the influence of the vampire Thibor Ferenczy.
   Element(s): SF/F.

162. ———. *Vamphyri!* New York: Tor, 1988. Paperback.
   Series: Necroscope No. 2.

Harry battles Yulian Bodescu, a man born with vampiric powers. Yulian attempts to take over the world with vampire monsters of his own making.
Element(s): SF/F.

163. ———. *The Source*. New York: Tor, 1989. Paperback.
Series: Necroscope No. 3.
In the Ural mountains the Soviets, through a horrific accident, create a supernatural portal that leads to the homeworld of the vampires. Harry uses this portal to enter the nightmare world known as Sunside/Starside, and fight the vampires on their own turf.
Element(s): SF/F.

164. ———. *Deadspeak*. New York: Tor, 1990. Paperback.
Series: Necroscope No. 4.
The ancient Janos Ferenczy, a vampire and magician, awakens from a long sleep and conjures an army of fiends which he plans to use to take over this world.
Element(s): SF/F.

165. ———. *Deadspawn*. New York: Tor, 1991. Paperback.
Series: Necroscope No. 5.
Harry tracks down an especially vicious killer, one who turns out to be a psychotic necromancer. He tortures his victims while alive and can still enjoy their torment after their death.
Element(s): SF/F.

166. ———. *Necroscope: The Lost Years*. New York: Tor, 1995. Hardcover.
Series: Necroscope No. 6.
This novel revisits Harry's early adult years and focuses on his search for his wife and young son who have vanished.
Element(s): SF/F.

167. ———. *Necroscope: the Lost Years II: Resurgence*. New York: Tor, 1996. Hardcover.
Series: Necroscope No. 7.
Harry falls in love with J. J. Mirlu, a beautiful lady who serves a powerful ancient Wamphyri lord.
Element(s): SF/F.

168. ———. Vampire World series.

During one of his many adventures, Harry Keogh spent time on Earth's parallel world, Sunside/Starside, where he fathered twin boys, Nathan and Nestor. This series focuses on them and takes place where the Necroscope series leaves off. The people of this world live in fear of the powerful Wamphyri, who use them as sources of food and perform ghastly experiments on them. The village in which Nestor and Nathan live is raided, and Nestor is carried off by a vampire. Nestor has long wanted to be one of the powerful Wamphyri. He gets his wish, but his human memories are fragmented. He believes his greatest enemy to be Nathan and eventually tracks his brother down and has him thrown through a mysterious gateway from which most believe there is no return. This gateway leads to earth, and here Nathan teams up with the British E-Branch in an attempt to stop a rogue group of Russian psychics and the ever-voracious vampires. As in the earlier series, there is a lot of heart-pounding adventure.

169. ———. *Blood Brothers*. New York: Tor, 1992. Hardcover.
Series: Vampire World No. 1.
Nathan travels through his world and eventually is thrown into the gate that connects Sunside/Starside with earth. Meanwhile Nestor becomes one of the powerful Wamphyri.
Element(s): SF/F.

170. ———. *The Last Aerie*. New York: Tor, 1993. Hardcover.
Series: Vampire World No. 2.
A sick and wounded Nestor hides in a cave and thinks back on how he came to be a Wamphyri. On earth Nathan joins with his father's old friends at E-Branch.
Element(s): SF/F.

171. ———. *Bloodwars*. New York: Tor, 1994. Hardcover.
Series: Vampire World No. 3.
Nathan returns to Sunside/Starside with weapons of earth—grenades, flamethrowers, and rocket launchers—to lead an attack on the Wamphyri.
Element(s): SF/F.

172. **MacMillan, Scott (author), and Katherine Kurtz (creator).**
Knights of the Blood: Vampyr-SS. New York: ROC, 1993.

Series: Knights of the Blood No. 1.

In the Holy Land of 1291, a group of crusader knights known as the Order of the Sword fight and destroy a band of vampires. The knights drink their enemies' blood in triumph and, to their horror, become vampires themselves. They withdraw to a castle in Europe.

Move forward to the twentieth century during World War II. An SS officer finds the castle and drinks the blood of one of the knights. The infection spreads anew. Now in modern day Los Angeles Detective John Drummond investigates a series of murders linked to the SS.

Element(s): Mystery, SF/F.

173. ———. *At Sword's Point*. New York: ROC, 1994. Paperback.
    Series: Knights of the Blood No. 2.
    The Nazi vampires are not yet vanquished. Drummond seeks out the Knights of the Sword and joins with them through a special ritual of blood drinking. With his newly acquired strength, he goes after the SS vampires. His pursuit, however, is hampered by, of all groups, Israel's spy agency, the Mossad.
    Element(s): SF/F.

174. **Martin, David.** *Tap, Tap*. New York: Random House, 1994.
    Hardcover. (Paperback. St. Martin's Paperbacks, 1996.)
    At age thirty-six, Roscoe Bird has a settled, relatively happy life with his wife Marianne. All that changes when Peter Tummelier, a friend from his teenage years, shows up one evening. Peter brings up the unhappy event of twenty years before when Roscoe's father committed suicide. He names those responsible for the father's despondency—people like the Burtons. People he is sure Roscoe must hate. Peter wants to know who else might be on that hate list. Then before taking his leave he makes this confession. He is a vampire and he has killed the Burtons. Roscoe discovers to his horror that at least the latter is true. Then other murders occur and all have a link to Roscoe. The setting is Washington, DC, and Florida.
    Element(s): Mystery.

175. **Martin, George R. R.** *Fevre Dream*. New York: Poseidon Press, 1982. Hardcover.
    Aristocrat and vampire Joshua York is traveling down the Mississippi River gathering members of his ancient, maligned race to free them from their heritage of bloodthirsty violence. First, however, he

must overcome a corrupt and powerful blood-master who awaits him in a crumbling Bayou plantation. His mortal friend and partner, riverboat captain Abner Marsh, risks everything to help Joshua.

Element(s): SF/F.

176. **Matheson, Richard.** *I Am Legend.* New York: Doubleday, 1954. Hardcover. (Various reprintings.)

This is one of the classics of vampire literature. A plague that has turned humans into vampires has swept the world. But one man, Robert Neville, survives. Every night he barricades himself inside his house prepared for the vampire attack, and by day he stakes as many of these undead as he can find. This story inspired George Romero's horror film, "Night of the Living Dead."

Films: *The Last Man on Earth* (1964); *The Omega Man* (1971); *Night of the Living Dead* (1968).

Element(s): SF/F

177. **McCammon, Robert R.** *They Thirst.* New York: Avon, 1981. Paperback. (Paperback. New York: Pocket Books, 1988.)

A big, scary book about a slow invasion of vampires that takes over the city of Los Angeles. Led by a monstrously evil master, the legion of undead seem to leave humans little chance of survival.

178. **Miller, Linda Lael.** Vampire Romance series.

In Miller's fantasy world, the undead can travel to different places and times, and they must contend with other paranormal beings including angels with attitude.

179. ———. *Forever and the Night.* New York: Berkley, 1993. Paperback.

Series: Vampire Romance No. 1.

Aidan Tremayne, a vampire for some two hundred years, longs to become human again. He meets Neely Wallace, a mortal woman who knows too much about a corrupt U.S. Senator and now has a price on her head. Their passionate attraction to each other is immediate. Aidan's friend and fellow vampire, Valerian, tries to help with Aidan's quest for mortality while Lisette, Queen of the Vampires, seeks revenge for Aidan's rejection of her.

Element(s): Category Romance, SF/F.

180. ———. *For All Eternity*. New York: Berkley, 1994. Paperback.
    Series: Vampire Romance No. 2.

Maeve, a vampire and Aidan's twin sister, discovers she is destined to replace the evil Lisette as queen of the undead. Meanwhile, Maeve has fallen in love with Calder Holbrook, a mortal physician with the Union Army during the Civil War. Eventually, he convinces her to make him a vampire, and, after the final battle with Lisette, they pledge their eternal love as wife and husband.
    Element(s): Category Romance, SF/F.

181. ———. *Time without End*. New York: Berkley Books, 1995. Paperback.
    Series: Vampire Romance No. 3.

The handsome Valerian, friend of Aidan and mentor to Maeve, has lived for six hundred years. Once each century he meets the reincarnation of the love of his life, Brenna, only to have her quickly torn from him in some terrible way. Now she appears in modern times as Daisy Chandler. Valerian must find a way to end the curse that keeps them apart and to destroy its perpetrator.
    Element(s): Category Romance, SF/F.

182. ———. *Tonight and Always*. New York: Berkley, 1996. Paperback.
    Series: Vampire Romance No. 4.

For the first time in history a child has been conceived by a vampire couple. Maeve and Calder have a child. Kristina, born in nineteenth-century London, is a mortal child with extraordinary powers. She lives for a hundred years without aging past thirty, until, that is, she meets her soulmate. But in a world filled with vampires, warlocks, and temperamental angels, the course of their romance does not run smoothly.
    Element(s): Category Romance, SF/F.

183. **Minns, Karen Marie Christa.** *Bloodsong*. Irvine, CA: Bluestocking Books, 1997. Paperback.

Ginny and Manilla meet at a prestigious women's college. When they become lovers Ginny's socially prominent family is horrified and threatens repercussions but the two women only cling more tightly to one another. Their love for each other is strong, and it needs to be when Darsen, a vampire of the vicious variety, enters the scene. She kills for the thrill but, when it comes to Ginny, Darsen would rather recruit her into the ranks of the undead.

Element(s): Romance (lesbian).

184. **Monahan, Brent.** *The Book of Common Dread.* New York: St. Martin's, 1993. Hardcover.

Vincent DeVilbiss, a five-hundred-year-old vampire, has been ordered by the mysterious evil entities who control him to find and destroy the ancient scrolls of Ahriman that now reside in a vaulted area of Princeton University Library. These scrolls contain metaphysical knowledge about the universe and the dark forces in it—knowledge that mankind must never discover. Unfortunately for DeVilbiss, his job proves more difficult than anticipated. Two Princeton librarians, Simon and Frederika, are more than worthy adversaries.

Element(s): Romance, SF/F.

185. ———. *The Blood of the Covenant.* New York: St. Martin's, 1995. Hardcover.

Sequel to *The Book of Common Dread.*

The Ahriman scrolls have been stolen from Princeton University Library by Simon and Frederika. These two are aided by a Roman Catholic priest (with the knowledge and support of the Pope) and a Princeton police detective. DeVilbiss has been put out of action, but the good guys must still outrun and outwit an especially vicious monster know only as the Vampire.

Element(s): Romance SF/F.

186. **Moore, Christopher.** *Bloodsucking Fiends: A Love Story.* New York: Simon & Schuster, 1995. Hardcover.

In San Francisco a vampire gets his jollies by creating fledglings and watching them flounder about before destroying them. But one fledgling is different. Jody is clever, a fast learner even at being a vampire. She meets Tommy, an aspiring writer who earns money by working the night shift at a supermarket. Their relationship becomes a loving one, and that bodes ill for the creator-vampire lurking in the shadows. This tale is told with lots of humor and gives a witty look at modern day life in the city.

Element(s): Humor, Romance.

187. **Murray, Doug.** *Blood Relations.* New York: HarperPrism, 1996. Paperback.

Publisher series: The World of Darkness: Vampire.

Val and Mariana had been lovers in the past. Now one of the Kindred's elders, a Methuselah, wants to use their feelings for each other as part of a plan to usurp control of New York City. This novel contains many scenes of violence and sadomasochism.

Element(s): Romance (dark).

188. **Nasaw, Jonathan.** *The World on Blood.* New York: Dutton, 1996. Hardcover.

In modern-day California a group of recovering addicts holds a meeting three nights a week at the Church of the Higher Power. Led by Nick Santos, the members of the group take turns telling their stories with some wonderfully hilarious psychobabble that parodies twelve-step programs. But these are no ordinary addicts. They are vampires. Here vampires are defined as humans with an exceptional metabolism that allows them to get high on blood. While high they have greatly heightened senses, extraordinary physical powers, and a slowdown in the aging process. But, best of all, the imbibed blood is a powerful aphrodisiac. Nick and the others in Vampires Anonymous (V.A.) have supposedly put their addiction aside. Jamey Whistler, however, thinks Nick's approach is all wrong, so he sets out, with the help of his witch-lover Selene, to destroy V.A.

Element(s): Humor, Romance.

189. ———. *Shadows.* New York: Dutton, 1997. Hardcover.

In this sequel to *The World on Blood* a hit man has been dispatched to destroy Jamey Whistler along with everything and everyone who ever had any importance in his life. The assassin, Aldo Striescu (also a vampire), is a former member of the dread Romanian secret police. His training in that organization has made him perfect for his new career. He almost succeeds in his task, but he had not counted on the power of Jamey's friend and lover, Selene. She gets her power from her long practice as a witch and from her profound love for Jamey. Although just as well-written as *The World on Blood*, *Shadows* has a darker, grittier quality.

Element(s): Mystery, Romance.

190. **Navarro, Yvonne.** *AfterAge.* New York: Bantam, 1993. Paperback.

The ancient vampire Anyelet loves modern-day Chicago, which teems with life. She decides to take it over by creating more beings like herself. Unfortunately she sets off a chain reaction which almost decimates this planet's human population and leaves vampires starving for sustenance. In the windy city, where it all began, a group of human survivors band together in an attempt to regain their world. Religious faith plays an important part in their struggle.

Element(s): Religion.

191. **Newman, Kim.** *Anno-Dracula*. New York: Carroll & Graf, 1993. Hardcover.

In this twist on Bram Stoker's *Dracula*, the Count easily survives Van Helsing's pitiful attempt to destroy him. He quickly goes on to win the hand of the widowed Queen Victoria. Vampires now hold sway in England, but not all are evil. In fact, one of the most enchanting characters in the story is Geneviève, a vampire older than Dracula who works to help the poor in the East End of London. It is Geneviève and her mortal lover, Charles Beauregard, who are Dracula's eventual undoing. This novel has a wonderful abundance of literary and historical characters.

Element(s): Dracula, Romance.

192. ———. *The Bloody Red Baron*. New York: Carroll & Graf, 1995. Hardcover.

Sequel to *Anno-Dracula*.

The world is at war, and Charles Beauregard now sits as a member of the Diogenes Club, the secret group that gathers intelligence for Britain. Cast out of Britain, Dracula has allied himself with Kaiser Wilhelm and commands the German armies, and he has a special interest in the fighting vampire flyers like the Bloody Red Baron, Manfred von Richtofen. These flying aces are attempting to take their vampiric powers to the maximum. As in *Anno-Dracula* Newman brings in a large cast of well-known characters, both historical and fictional. In this alternate world many leaders and common folk are vampires. Among the former is Winston Churchill.

Element(s): Dracula, Romance.

193. **Nickles, Jason (aka T. Lucien Wright).** *Immortal*. New York: Zebra, 1996. Paperback.

At an archaeological site a buried box reveals what seems to be a wax dummy dressed up as vampire. The scientist in charge gives the figure to his father David Kane who promptly dubs the new find Martin and takes it back to his New York office. It turns out, however, that Mar-

tin really is a vampire, and now that he is back in the world he can begin transforming others—lots of them. David's daughter Emily and her
friend Ray team up with another vampire to stop Martin.

194. **Pierce, Meredith Ann.** The Darkangel Trilogy.
Although all the books in this trilogy are listed, only the first book
has an important vampiric element.

195. ———. *The Darkangel*. Boston: Little Brown, 1982. Hardcover.
(Paperback. New York: Tor, 1984.)
Series: The Darkangel Trilogy, Book one.
This story is set on earth's moon in a distant future where creatures
like gargoyles, witches, and vampires have sprung from human bio-
engineering. A vampire has kidnapped a woman. Her young servant,
Aerial, seeks to destroy him, but the vampire (also called the darkangel)
is very beautiful and, Aerial discovers, not completely evil.
Element(s): Romance, SF/F.

196. ———. A *Gathering of Gargoyles*. Boston: Little Brown, 1984.
Hardback. (Paperback. New York: Tor, 1984.)
Series: The Darkangel Trilogy, Book two.

197. ———. *The Pearl of the Soul of the World*. Boston: Little Brown,
1990. Hardcover.
Series: The Darkangel Trilogy, Book three.

198. **Pike, Christopher.** *The Season of Passage*. New York: Tor, 1993.
Paperback.
In the year 2002 the Russians sent a manned expedition to Mars.
After a few days all communication with the cosmonauts ceased. Two
years later the Americans send their own expedition. Shortly before taking off, the astronauts are given a secret briefing in which they are shown
a photograph which appears to show a footprint—one of nonhuman origin. A member of the American team, physician Lauren Wagner, begins having nightmares. Once her team lands on Mars and discovers the
terrible fate that overtook the Russians, the reality of daily life begins to
mimic her nightmare world. Meanwhile, on earth, her sister Jennifer
feels compelled to write a dark fantasy, one that may hold the key to the
monstrous, vampiric entity that stalks human travelers on Mars.
Element(s): SF/F.

199. **Powers, Tim.** *The Stress of Her Regard.* New York: Ace, 1989. Hardcover. (A signed limited edition of this book was privately printed by Charnel House.)

Michael Crawford enters the nightmarish world of the lamia one dark and stormy night when he slips his fiancée's wedding ring on the statue of a nude woman. The morning after his wedding to Julia, he awakes to find his bride's mutilated body next to him in bed. He flees this horror and encounters John Keats who explains that a vampire, or lamia, has a firm hold on him. Soon after, Michael goes to Switzerland where Byron, Shelley and John Polidori become a part of his struggle to free himself from his curse.

200. **Reeves-Stevens, Garfield.** *Bloodshift.* New York: Popular Library, 1990. Paperback. (Author copyright is 1981.)

In this complex adventure, Adrienne St. Claire leaves the vampire Covenant in Europe and flees to a secret destination in North America. Her departure is looked upon by several groups, all with different agendas, as an act that could bring terrible consequences. She is pursued by Jesuit priests and tracked by an American military intelligence unit. To add to her woes, the vampire Covenant that she has betrayed intends to make sure she is destroyed. To do this they hire Granger Helman, a former freelance hit man, who had hoped to retire from his profession and put killing behind him.

Element(s): Mystery, SF/F.

201. **Reines, Kathryn.** *The Kiss.* New York: Avon, 1996. Paperback.

In 1938 Americans Rebecca and Richard flee the Nazis of Berlin only to find themselves in the clutches of two lusty vampires, the Count and Countess Viroslav. This novel has scene after scene of sensuous passion. Only slowly is the thoroughly evil nature of the two immortals revealed. A story for fans of erotic fiction.

Element(s): Romance (erotic).

202. **Rice, Anne.** *Interview with the Vampire.* New York: Knopf, 1976. Hardcover. (Paperback. New York: Ballantine, 1997.)

Series: The Vampire Chronicles No. 1.

In this dark, sensuous tale Louis tells of his life as he has lived it for the past two hundred years. Louis has never lost his human soul and never accepted the necessity of taking human life. The torment he suffers and the sinister underworld of vampires all come forth as Louis talks to a young mortal reporter. For Louis, his creator, Lestat, is the person-ification of evil.

203.   ———. *The Vampire Lestat*. New York: Knopf, 1985. Hardcover. (Paperback. New York: Ballantine, 1997.)
Series: The Vampire Chronicles No. 2.
Here we see the story from Lestat's point of view, and, although he shows himself to be bold and egotistical, he is hardly the sinister en-tity depicted by Louis. Lestat, however, pushes through boundaries that no vampire had ever dared before, and he catches the attention of the oldest of the undead, Akasha. For thousands of years she has been in a sleep-like state. But this ancient beauty is aroused by Lestat's music and extraordinary spirit. Thanks to Lestat the Queen has risen.

204.   ———. *The Queen of the Damned*. New York: Knopf, 1988. Hardcover. (Paperback. New York: Ballantine, 1997.)
Series: The Vampire Chronicles No. 3.
Akasha has awakened and walks the land with Lestat caught in her spell. She brings death to any she considers an enemy. Now, a group of immortals, many almost as old as the Queen herself, have gathered, for only they have the power to stop her.

205.   ———. *The Tale of the Body Thief*. New York: Knopf, 1992. Hardcover. (Paperback. New York: Ballantine, 1997.)
Series: The Vampire Chronicles No. 4.
Raglan James, genius, con artist, and psychic, convinces Lestat to trade bodies temporarily. This gives Lestat the chance to experience mortal pleasures no longer available to him, and James can know the power of the vampire. Much to his chagrin, Lestat learns James is not to be trusted. The fact is, James never planned to give Lestat back his body. He is a body thief.

206.   ———. *Memnoch the Devil*. New York: Knopf, 1995. Hardcover. (Paperback. New York: Ballantine, 1997.)
Series: The Vampire Chronicles No. 5.
Lestat feels real fear for the first time in centuries. He is being fol-lowed by what he senses to be a diabolical presence. When he is at last confronted by this nemesis, he finds himself face to face with Satan, who

prefers to be called Memnoch. He wants Lestat to understand why he is at war with God and why other angels question God's divine plan for humanity. Lestat witnesses the great philosophical debate between God and Memnoch the Devil.

207. **Rice, Jeff.** *The Night Stalker*. New York: Pocket Books, 1973. Paperback. (Retitled: *The Kolchak Papers #1: The Night Stalker*. Massapequa Park, New York: Cinemaker, 1993. Paperback.)

Hard-nosed, irascible investigative reporter Carl Kolchak is convinced that a serial killer on the loose in Las Vegas is a vampire, but he has a hard time convincing the incompetent police that he is right. The vampire is a rather nasty brute named Janos Skorzeny. He not only kills for blood; he also keeps a personal blood bank of victims imprisoned in his hideout. This book is the basis for the TV movie *The Night Stalker*, starring Darren McGavin.

Film and TV series.

208. **Romkey, Michael.** *I, Vampire*. New York: Fawcett, 1990. Paperback.

This is David Parker's journal of his first year as a vampire. The year is 1989. He was transformed by the Russian Grand Duchess Tatiana (a daughter of Nicholas II) and has found a mentor in the musical genius Mozart. Other famous and infamous persons, such as Lucrezia Borgia, Rasputin, and Prince Victor Albert, make vampiric appearances in this novel. Now alone in Paris, David works to strengthen his vampire powers, but his efforts are thwarted by the sinister presence of another undead, one whose evil is palpable and whose powers are greater than David can ever hope to obtain.

209. ———. *The Vampire Papers*. New York: Fawcett, 1994. Paperback.

In this complex sequel to *I, Vampire*, David Parker now belongs to a select group of vampires known as the Illuminati—a benevolent group that believes it wrong to kill mortals. He has been given the task of stopping a serial killer rampaging in New York. The killer, Becker Thorne, is a vampire of extraordinary power who revels in his sadistic killings. This crazed nosferatu follows the messages of the godlike entity Neon, who sends him on missions to punish the wicked. David follows Thorne to Jerusalem, Mississippi, where Thorne plans a terrible vengeance against the entire town.

210. ———. *The Vampire Princess*. New York: Fawcett, 1996. Paperback.
 Sequel to *The Vampire Papers*.
 David has become the lover of Principessa Nicoletta Vittorini di Medusa, a centuries-old vampiress of great beauty and cruelty who has seduced him from the ways of the Illuminati. David's conscience reasserts itself, and he makes a vain attempt to break away. Her hold, however, is too great. She insists he accompany her on the maiden voyage of a luxury liner named the Atlantic Princess. David is helpless to stop the bloodbath planned by Nicoletta on the passengers. Several chapters of the novel are in the form of diary entries by Nicoletta in which she tries to justify her sadistic nature.

211. **Rudorff, Raymond.** *The Dracula Archives*. New York: Arbor House, 1971. Hardcover. (Paperback. New York: Pocketbook, 1973.)
 In this eerie, complex tale we witness the merging of two infamous houses: those of Vlad Tepes and the bloodthirsty Countess Elizabeth Bathory. The story is told through letters and diary entries in a style reminiscent of Stoker.
 Element(s): Bathory, Dracula.

212. **Rusch, Kristine Kathryn.** *Sins of the Blood*. New York: Dell, 1994. Paperback.
 In this alternate world vampires exist among humans, and in some American states, like Wisconsin, they can be legally eradicated. Cammie is an eradicator for the Westrina Center. On an assignment she breaks into a vampire's apartment and drives a stake through his heart. To her surprise and horror, there is a young child living there who is devastated at her daddy's murder. This incident awakens in Cammie frightening childhood memories that she had repressed. Her father, too, had been a vampire, a cruel man who killed her human mother. She also had a little brother, Ben, whom she had tried to protect. She decides to leaves the Center and go in search of Ben. Meanwhile, in alternating chapters, the reader meets Ben, whose hereditary vampiric nature has only recently become apparent. He revels in these powers. This is an intense and sometimes unnerving story.

213. **Saberhagen, Fred.** Dracula series.
 Count Dracula has had a bad press thanks to Bram Stoker. In this

series of adventures, readers learn what a charming, caring fellow he really is. Several of the novels are predicated on Dracula's concern for the Southerland family. These are Mina Harker's modern-day descendents, and they seem to attract dangers from the supernatural realm. Luckily for them they have a protector, and he first appears as such in *An Old Friend of the Family* (see #216).

214. ———. *The Dracula Tape*. New York: Warner, 1975. Paperback.
    (New York: Tor, 1989.)
    Series: Dracula No. 1.
    In a series of tape recordings Dracula (Vlad Tepes) tells his version of events involving Jonathan Harker, Mina, Lucy Westenra, Van Helsing and the others made famous in Stoker's story. Vlad insists that he did not do any of the dastardly deeds ascribed to him in the aforementioned infamous tale. In fact he is a very nice guy and tries to help others whenever he can. Certainly his feelings of love for Mina are genuine. This is a wry, witty rebuttal to the vampire classic.
    Element(s): Dracula.

215. ———. *The Holmes-Dracula File*. New York: Ace, 1978. Paperback.
    Series: Dracula No. 2.
    It is the year 1897. One night, while walking the streets of London, Dracula is hit from behind and over the head with a stout piece of wood. Steel or iron would have done no damage, but wood causes horrendous harm to a vampire. When he awakens he finds himself prisoner in some dank room and with no memory of who or what he is. Meanwhile Sherlock Holmes has been hired by a young woman to find her fiancée. The two divergent story lines converge soon enough because both involve a terrible creature called the Giant Rat of Sumatra. The reader also discovers that Dracula and Holmes are almost identical in appearance.
    Element(s): Dracula, Mystery.

216. ———. *An Old Friend of the Family*. New York: Ace, 1979. Hardcover. (Paperback. New York: Tor, 1987.)
    Series: Dracula No. 3.
    A terrible evil has overtaken the Southerland family. Kate has been murdered, but is not quite dead, and her brother has been kidnapped. Matriarch Clarissa turns to her grandmother Mina's friend, a vampire who calls himself Dr. Emil Corday. The reader quickly figures

out that this is actually Dracula. He must confront the monster behind this terrible deed and soon discovers that he was the target all along. The setting is contemporary Chicago and features police detective Joe Keogh, who will appear in other stories in this series.

Element(s): Dracula, Mystery.

217. ———. *Thorn*. New York: Tor, 1990. Paperback.
    Series: Dracula No. 4.

The Thorn of the title is Jonathan Thorn, Dracula's current name or at least the one used in this adventure. There are alternating chapters between Thorn's modern-day story and a segment of time when Vlad Dracula was a living, breathing human being. In today's world Thorn becomes involved in the disappearance of a young woman from a wealthy family. Her name is Helen. Five hundred years ago Vlad took as his second wife Helen, sister of the Hungarian King Matthias. It is no coincidence that both women have the same name and resemble one another.

Element(s): Dracula, Mystery.

218. ———. *A Matter of Taste*. New York: Tor, 1990. Hardcover. (Paperback. New York: Tor, 1992.)
    Series: Dracula No. 6.

A vicious gang of vampires is trying to kill Vlad (here known as Matthew Maule). John Southerland knows Matthew's nature and has the difficult task of protecting him from some truly evil nosferatu. Intertwined with the main plot is an accounting of how in the distant past Dracula came to his vampiric state.

Element(s): Dracula.

219. ———. *A Question of Time*. New York: Tor, 1992. Paperback.
    Series: Dracula No. 7.

In 1991 Cathy Brainard disappears in the Grand Canyon, and in 1933 Jake Rezner becomes trapped in a time vortex located in the same area. Both people are connected to sculptor Edgar Tyrell who is also a vampire—the evil kind. Southerland family members, along with family friend Dracula, search for the missing and battle the malevolent Mr. Tyrell.

Element(s): Dracula, SF/F.

220. ———. *Seance for a Vampire*. New York: Tor, 1994. Hardcover.
    Series: Dracula No. 8.

Sherlock Holmes and Dracula are partnered again. This time an evil vampire terrorizes a family whose daughter has entered the realm of the nosferatu. Some fake mediums get involved, much to their deep regret. The story is told alternatively by Dracula and Holmes's pal Dr. Watson.

Element(s): Dracula.

221. ———. *A Sharpness on the Neck*. New York: Tor, 1996. Hardcover.
Series: Dracula No. 9.

In 1996 a young couple named Radcliffe are hunted by Radu, vampire brother of Vlad Dracula. Radu wishes to avenge himself on the descendants of Philip Radcliffe, who saved the life of Vlad and thus earned Radu's eternal enmity. The life-saving event took place during the French Revolution, and there are some rather grisly scenes with the infamous guillotine.

Element(s): Dracula, History.

222. **Sackett, Jeffrey.** *Blood of the Impaler*. New York: Bantam, 1989. Paperback.

Malcolm Harker carries tainted blood from his great-grandmother Mina. She was forced to drink Dracula's blood, and the evil inherent in it was passed along to her descendents. At least that is what Malcolm's grandfather, Quincy, tells him. Quincy sees his grandson beginning to suffer afflictions with which he too had wrestled—aversion to sunlight, energy peaks at night, and a longing for human blood. Adherence to Christian tenets, specifically the taking of holy communion, is the only way to keep the evil at bay, says the grandfather. He also insists that Bram Stoker wrote the truth. Malcolm is not sure what to believe, so with two friends he sets sail for England. Using Stoker's *Dracula* as their guide they trace people and places and find to their growing horror that Quincy is right. What is worse, they come to realize that the blood of Dracula, who was in life Vlad the Impaler, is stronger than any of them had imagined.

Element(s): Dracula, Religion.

223. **Saxon, Peter.** *The Vampires of Finistere*. New York: Berkley, 1970. Paperback.
Series: The Guardians No. 4.

The Guardians are a group of mortal investigators organized to combat evil. In this episode they must find a young woman who disap-

peared in a remote French seaside village. One of the evil beings whom
they confront is a sea-dwelling vampire. When she takes human form,
she has an intense appetite for sex as well as blood.
    Element(s): SF/F.

224. **Scarborough, Elizabeth.** *The Goldcamp Vampire.* New York:
        Bantam, 1987. Paperback.
    Valentine Lovelace, the heroine of this lighthearted tale, heads for
the gold rush madness of the Yukon with Sasha, mistress of her recently
deceased father. It will be an adventure for them both. They become involved not only with a vampire of rather roguish charm but also with a
werewolf and a weremoose.
    Element(s): Humor, Romance.

225. **Shayne, Maggie.** Wings of the Night series.
    In Maggie Shayne's vampire world certain humans are called the
Chosen, which means that they carry a rare blood antigen necessary for
transformation to the vampire state. These Chosen are secretly guarded
by vampires, to which they have a psychic link. A government group that
knows about vampires and the Chosen is the CIA's Division of Paranormal Investigations (DPI). The agents of DPI hunt these individuals
so that their scientists can study them. The methodology used by the re-
searchers is far from humane although the books carry no graphic de-
scriptions. This is after all a romance series and includes some steamy
sex scenes. Characters from the various books tend to turn up at some
point in all of the novels. (*See also* the novella *Beyond Twilight* #575.)

226. ———. *Twilight Phantasies.* New York: Silhouette, 1993. Paper-
        back.
    Series: Wings of the Night No. 1.
    Publisher series: Silhouette Shadows No. 18.
    Eric Marquand became a vampire more than two centuries ago.
Now living on Long Island, he feels a strong attraction to Tamara Dey—
one of the Chosen—and that feeling is returned. Danger for the two
comes from Tamara's mortal guardian, who, unknown to her, is one of
DPI's vampire hunters.
    Element(s): Category Romance, SF/F.

227. ———. *Twilight Memories.* New York: Silhouette, 1994. Paper-
        back.

Series: Wings of the Night No. 2.

Publisher series: Silhouette Shadows No. 30.

The vampire Roland hides the young Jameson, one of the Chosen, in a small French village, but a DPI agent has followed them. The lovely vampiress Rhiannon warns Roland of the danger. For centuries Rhiannon has loved Roland, but he has held his feelings in check. That, of course, will change. They are aided in their attempt to protect Jameson by Tamara and Eric.

Element(s): Category Romance, SF/F.

228. ———. *Twilight Illusions*. New York: Silhouette, 1994. Paperback.

Series: Wings of the Night No. 3.

Publisher series: Silhouette Shadows No. 47.

Shannon suspects a popular magician named Damien of killing her best friend. Not true, she learns, but Damien does have a secret. He is an ancient vampire, one who has deliberately kept himself away from his kind. That changes when he meets Shannon, one of the Chosen to whom he is irresistibly drawn. Now they both face danger from two sources—a rogue vampire and DPI agent Stephen Bachman.

Element(s): Category Romance, SF/F.

229. ———. *Born in Twilight*. New York: Silhouette, March 1997. Paperback.

Series: Wings of the Night No. 4.

Jameson, now an adult and still in his status of Chosen, has been captured by DPI. They wish to use him for a new experiment. His sperm will be used on a newly transformed female vampire to create a child. The experiment works, but now Jameson and Angelica, the child's mother, must use all their resources to rescue their baby daughter from the clutches of DPI.

Element(s): Category Romance, SF/F.

230. **Shepard, Lucius.** *The Golden*. New York: Bantam, 1993. Paperback.

The collective of vampires known as the Family has gathered at Castle Banat for the decanting of exquisite mortal blood. For three centuries, specially selected bloodlines had produced the Golden, and now all would partake of her essence. But before that could happen, someone brutally murders the Golden and drains every bit of her blood. It becomes the task of Michel Beheim, formerly chief of detectives of the Paris police force and new member of the Family, to find the killer.

Element(s): Mystery, Romance.

231. **Siciliano, Sam.** *Blood Feud.* New York: Pinnacle, 1993. Paperback.

Mary never got over the loss of her brother Alex. She knows the identity of the woman he was last seen with. Now six years later, she sees the woman again with her brother's friend Steve. Then private investigator Roland Smith enters the picture. He convinces Mary that her brother was murdered by the vampire Françoise de Rambouillet, and that his client also lost someone to this same nosferatu. He invites her along on his mission to kill Madame Rambouillet as she sleeps by day in her coffin. Mary agrees, but when she tells Steve as well as her friend, Catholic priest Fred Martin, they both insist on going along. The plan to stake the vampire during the day seems straightforward enough, but, in fact, all of them are walking into a trap.

Element(s): Religion.

232. **Simmons, Dan.** *Children of the Night.* New York: G.P. Putnam's, 1992. Hardcover. (New York: Warner, 1993. Paperback.)

Dr. Kate Neuman is a physician working for the Centers for Disease Control (CDC). She is one of many sent on a humanitarian mission to post-Ceaucescu Romania. Many children, mostly orphans, are desperately ill, and Kate does what she can, in her short stay, to save them. One child in particular gains her attention. He is an abandoned baby, seven months old, who suffers from an unknown disease that almost kills him. Only frequent blood transfusions allow him to rally. Kate decides to adopt the little boy, whom she names Joshua, and bring him to the United States, where she can use the resources of CDC to save his life. Her research shows that Joshua has a peculiar mechanism that uses blood to bring about rapid cellular changes and healing. Meanwhile, Vlad Dracula has returned to Romania to die. He has an heir, a baby who carries his genes, and who will be invested during a special ceremony. But something has gone wrong, and Dracula's minions are afraid to tell him the child has disappeared.

(*See* #527 "All Dracula's Children" for the short story that forms the first part of this novel.)

Element(s): Dracula, SF/F.

233. **Simmons, Wm. Mark.** *One Foot in the Grave.* New York: Baen, 1996. Paperback.

Christopher Csejthe has lost his appetite and can no longer stand the sunlight. He thinks he is dying. But the truth is he is an anomaly—a human slowly transforming into a vampire. One enclave leader of the undead feels a dangerous being such as this must be eliminated. Another, however, is willing to give him protection. In fact this powerful nosferatu, Stephan, makes Chris an offer: stay in his territory or die—permanently. Stephan also allows a human medical doctor to study Chris's condition in the hope of finding answers to many questions about vampirism. This story is narrated by Chris, who comes forth with witty repartee even while in some rather horrifying situations.

Note: Vampire aficionados will recognize Chris's family name as that of Elizabeth Bathory's castle; however, that connection is not mentioned in this novel.

Element(s): SF/F.

234. **Smith, Robert Arthur.** *Vampire Notes.* New York: Fawcett, 1989. Paperback.

George, a producer with a recent run of theater flops, is hired by the rich and eccentric Mr. Mornay to produce a play. George's happiness turns to horror when he begins to suspect that Mornay is a vampire and that the new play will be used for a diabolical purpose.

235. **Somtow, S. P.** Timmy Valentine series.

The central character of this trilogy is Timmy Valentine, a prepubescent 2,000-year-old vampire and, in today's world, a rock star of immense popularity. He has also reached a point of personal crisis. His developing conscience leads him to sympathize with his human victims and have feelings of guilt for the vampire predators that many of them become. While trying to come to terms with evil he finds within himself, Timmy must also protect himself from a group of thrill-seeking vampire hunters who have some potent magic on their side. At one point Timmy gives up his vampire essence to a lookalike named Angel Todd, a character with a truly demonic nature. There is a host of subplots and a plethora of characters, plus no end of graphic violence. But, even with the splatter punk approach found in many scenes, there is, oddly enough, a feeling of spirituality to the entire work.

236. ———. *Vampire Junction*. New York: Berkley, 1984. Hardcover.
(New York: Tor, 1991 Paperback.)
Series: Timmy Valentine No. 1.
A group of Satanists, who call themselves the Gods of Chaos, are angry at Timmy because some years ago he broke up their attempt at a human sacrifice. They vow to track him down and destroy him.

237. ———. *Valentine*. New York: Tor, 1992. Paperback.
Series: Timmy Valentine No. 2.
The events in this sequel take place ten years later. Timmy has entered an alternate world where he is tormented by the powers of black magician Simone Arleta. The key to his freedom lies with Angel Todd.

238. ———. *Vanitas: Escape from Vampire Junction*. New York: Tor, 1995. Hardcover.
Series: Timmy Valentine No. 3.
Timmy has become mortal by giving his vampire powers to Angel Todd. Unfortunately Angel uses these powers in a most destructive, hideous way. Timmy's friends help him find Angel, but only Timmy can confront this creature and put a stop to the terror he has unleashed on the world.

239. **Spruill, Steven.** *Rulers of Darkness*. New York: St. Martin's, 1995. Hardcover.
Police detective Merrick Chapman does not believe in vampires. He prefers to think of his kind as hemophages, immortals who live on human blood and have an almost overwhelming urge to kill their victims. Merrick has learned to suppress that urge, and he hunts and destroys those who will not. Here the killer he stalks is his own son, Zane. But Zane is fighting back by threatening a mortal woman loved by Merrick, Dr. Katherine O'Keefe. Katherine, a hematologist, has gotten a sample of hemophage blood and is close to exposing the secret of this mutant group. Not even Merrick will allow that. The setting for this fast-paced story is modern-day Washington, D.C.
Element(s): SF/F, Mystery.

240. ———. *Daughter of Darkness*. New York: Doubleday, 1997. Hardcover.
The sequel to *Rulers of Darkness* takes place ten years later and focuses on Jenn, Zane's biological daughter and inheritor of his hemophage

gene. Her grandfather, Merrick, has shown her how to survive by transfusing human blood, and how to control the instinct to kill for that blood. Zane wants Jenn to be a killer like himself, and he will do anything to force her to his way of thinking, even if it requires making it look to the police as if she were a murderer.

Element(s): SF/F.

241. **St. George, Margaret.** *Love Bites*. New York: Harlequin, 1995.

Trevor d'Laine, the radio talk show host with the warm, sexy voice, bills himself as the Prince of Darkness and claims to be a bona fide vampire. Kay Erickson is sure this is nonsense — just part of the theatrics that go with show business. She applies for a job as his assistant. The interview is held in the middle of the night, and he insists on calling her his Renfield. She slowly realizes Trevor is exactly what he says he is and that he relishes every minute of his existence. Like most of his species, he is a nice person. He has never killed anyone and, in fact, now belongs to a vampire group that gets their blood supply without attacking humans. Not all vampires, though, agree with this attitude. Vampires are to be feared, they believe. This group causes quite a few problems for Kay and Trevor, who have fallen in love.

Element(s): Category Romance.

242. **Stableford, Brian.** *The Empire of Fear*. New York: Ballantine, 1993. Paperback. (New York: Carroll & Graf, 1988. Hardcover.)

This alternative history and vampire tale begins in seventeenth-century England, which is ruled by the vampire Prince Richard the Lionheart, with the help of other aristocratic undead. The mortal Noell Cordery carries on the secret, forbidden work begun by his scientist father — the search for the true cause of vampirism, with hopes of eradicating it.

(*See* #425, "The Man Who Loved the Vampire Lady" for the short story that makes up the first part of this novel.)

Element(s): SF/F.

243. **Steakley, John.** *Vampire$*. New York: ROC, 1990. Paperback.

Jack Crow leads a team, backed by the Vatican, which hunts down and kills vampires in the modern-day world. It is a terrifying and often deadly job, but this group of adventurers never backs away from its assignment to stamp out the evil undead.

244. **Stevens, Amanda.** *Dark Obsession.* New York: Silhouette, 1994. Paperback.
Publisher series: Silhouette Shadows No. 48.
The sister of horror writer Erin Ramsey has been murdered, all blood drained from her body. Investigating police detective Nick Slade knows the killer. A few years before, the vampire Drake D'Angelo had turned Nick's fiancée into one of the undead. Nick destroyed the thing she had become and almost did the same to Drake. Now Drake seeks revenge. He will kill as many people as possible before going after his ultimate target—Erin, the woman with whom Nick has fallen in love.
Element(s): Category Romance.

245. **Stoker, Bram.** *Dracula.* Westminster: Constable, 1897. First American edition, New York: Doubleday & McClure, 1899. Hardcover. Continuously in print.
Stoker's Dracula has come to personify what fiction readers of this century identify as a vampire: an undead creature who lives on human blood, makes his rounds at night, has superhuman strength, casts no reflection in a mirror, hates garlic, fears crosses and holy water, and can change into a bat, a wolf, or mist at will. Even though these traits are familiar and countless films have been made about Dracula, this powerfully written novel still rouses fear in even the most jaded heart. Through the journals, diaries, and letters of those besieged by this evil count, the horror builds as Dracula's plan to move his stronghold from Transylvania to Victorian England and create a new unlife for himself advances.
For anyone not familiar with the story, a look at the various protagonists can be useful because they often show up in other vampire stories—sometimes individually but often as an ensemble.

Count Dracula—a centuries-old vampire of immense evil who has lived his many years in the Carpathian mountains of Transylvania, causing endless grief and terror to nearby residents. He plans to leave his ancestral home for England's shores.
Jonathan Harker—a young solicitor who travels to Transylvania at the behest of the Count in order to help him prepare for the move to England. Jonathan soon realizes he is not only in the presence of a terrible evil, but worse, is a prisoner in imminent peril for his life and soul.
Lucy Westenra—a lively, pretty young woman with three handsome suitors. She is also Dracula's first English victim.

Lucy's suitors: Arthur Holmwood—heir of Lord Godalming and the winner in the contest to win Lucy's hand; Quincey P. Morris—an American from Texas; John Seward—a doctor in charge of a nearby lunatic asylum. When Lucy becomes ill and does not respond to treatment, John sends for his former mentor Dr. Van Helsing in hopes that a cure can be found for her.

Mina Harker (née Murray)—fiancée and later wife of Jonathan, she is also a close friend of Lucy's. After Lucy's death, Mina becomes the object of Dracula's attention. He wants her for his bride. But the scheme is interrupted by Dr. Abraham Van Helsing. Still, Mina has drunk some of Dracula's blood and now has a psychic link to him. This link is used to track him when he flees.

Dr. Abraham Van Helsing—An expert in obscure diseases sent for from Amsterdam by John Seward. Van Helsing becomes suspicious of what lies behind Lucy's illness but is unable to save her. It is Van Helsing who then convinces the other men—Harker and Lucy's suitors—that a vampire is at work and must be hunted down and destroyed.

Renfield—a patient in Dr. Seward's asylum. Renfield practices his own brand of entomology: after quietly studying flies and spiders, he eats them. For a time he becomes the human servant of Dracula.

Element(s): Dracula (of course).

246. **Stoker, Bram, and editor Leonard Wolf.** *The Essential Dracula: The Definitive Edition of Bram Stoker's Classic Novel.* New York: Plume, 1993. Paperback.

To enhance the atmosphere of this classic horror story, extensive notes, arranged close to the pertinent text, give glimpses into late nineteenth-century Europe as well as expound on the vampire myth. Also included is the deleted first chapter of the original novel. It is often anthologized as the short story "Dracula's Guest." A bibliography of sources used by the editor in preparation of this book plus a brief filmography is included.

Element(s): Dracula.

247. **Strieber, Whitley.** *The Hunger.* New York: William Morrow, 1981. Hardcover. (New York: Pocket Books, 1982. Paperback.)

Miriam Blaylock is a vampire, one of a race that was never human. Throughout her long life she has had companions—humans whom she transformed so that she would have someone with which to share her life. Others of her race have been hunted and killed almost to extinction, and it has been many years since she has seen one of her own. Miriam has a desperate need for love and companionship, but the humans who survive transformation only live the vampire life for a few hundred years. Now, however, in the twentieth century, a researcher, Dr. Sarah Roberts, may have stumbled across a way to slow or even stop the aging process. Miriam sees this as a possible answer to the terrible loss she feels each time one of her lovers meets his or her end. She sets out to seduce Sarah, use the new method for her own ends, and then transform Sarah as her next companion.

Film: The Hunger (1983).

Element(s): SF/F.

248. **Swiniarski, S. A.** *Raven.* New York: DAW, 1996.

Kane Tyler's ex-wife has been brutally murdered and his teenage daughter is in terrible danger. His nightmare began when a mobster hired him to find his own missing daughter. She was somehow involved with a man named Childe, a man who personified evil. Now Kane finds his body changed and his memory gone. Slowly images of his recent past return, and he becomes aware that he has been transformed into a vampire. Childe holds the key to all that has happened, but stopping this creature may prove difficult even for a former policeman and new member of the Covenant. The setting for this story is Cleveland, Ohio, in the dead of winter. Brrrr!

Element(s): Mystery, SF/F.

249. **Taylor, Karen E.** The Vampire Legacy series.

Deirdre Griffin lives and works in Manhattan. For ten years, she has owned a successful clothing business, Griffin Designs. As a nonaging vampire, she knows it is time to think about moving on before people become suspicious of her eternal youth. But before that can happen, her life becomes incredibly complicated by several murders. Victims are found drained of blood, and all of them are acquaintances of Deirdre. One of the detectives sent to investigate the crimes is Mitch Greer. Soon convinced of her innocence, Mitch falls in love with Deirdre, and that love is returned. Many scenes throughout the series are devoted to their passionate lovemaking. Eventually the murders are solved, but this only leads to more complications, including Deirdre's discovery of the vampire who transformed her 150 years before plus an entire underground world of vampires.

250. ———. *Blood Secrets*. New York: Zebra, 1994. Paperback.
    Series: Vampire Legacy No. 1.
    Deirdre and Mitch meet when he questions her about the homicides. They fall in love and work together to solve the mystery. During the investigation Deirdre discovers the identity of the vampire who changed her.
    Element(s): Mystery, Romance.

251. ———. *Bitter Blood*. New York: Zebra, 1994. Paperback.
    Series: Vampire Legacy No. 2.
    Mitch and Deirdre plan to wed, but their survival is now threatened by a secret society of vampires called the Cadre. This group threatens to destroy them both because Deirdre had once killed one of her own kind.
    Element(s): Mystery, Romance.

252. ———. *Blood Ties*. New York: Zebra, 1995. Paperback.
    Series: Vampire Legacy No. 3.
    A rogue vampire roams the streets of New York and must be stopped. The Cadre assigns the task of tracking him down to Deirdre and Mitch, who is now himself a vampire.
    Element(s): Mystery, Romance.

253. **Tedford, William.** *Liquid Diet*. New York: Diamond, 1992. Paperback.
    High School senior Troy Davidson lives in a rural area with his Aunt Audrey. He has no memory of the parents who died when he was young. He knows that he is different from others around him. Since puberty he has had a nighttime persona that sends him out to satisfy a hunger for human blood. Usually, he satisfies his cravings by seducing women while they dream. Rarely does he kill. His teenage neighbor, Melissa French, has always been fascinated by Troy because he, like she, is a social outsider. Then, she begins to feel strange stirrings of change within herself and wakes up one morning with blood on her lips. Meanwhile a coroner in this isolated county is investigating several cases in which elderly people have died of complete blood loss.
    Element(s): SF/F.

254. **Tem, Melanie.** *Desmodus*. New York: Dell, 1995. Paperback.
    A surreal look at the vampires who share the world with us. The Desmodus clan is getting ready for the annual migration south. Joel tells

the story from his perspective as an inferior male. Women are the superior ones among vampires, or so Joel, the narrator of this story, has been taught to believe. He is soon to learn some shocking, disturbing truths.

255. **Tilton, Lois.** *Darkness on the Ice.* New York: Pinnacle, 1993. Paperback.

The story takes place during WW II. Only a very few in the Nazi high command know of the existence of the vampire Wolff. An agreement has been reached with him: If he helps the Nazis to protect a vital weather station high above the arctic circle, Wolff will have not only four months of blissful nights, but also the deed to his lost ancestral lands in the Carpathian mountains. At the weather station the German soldiers become suspicious of this man who never eats and feels no pain from the Arctic cold. Meanwhile the Americans know this weather station exists but not its exact location. A dogsled team is dispatched to find it. Wolff sees these Americans not so much as enemies of the Reich but as a necessary food supply. He stalks them like the predator he is.

256. **Vitola, Denise.** *The Winter Man.* New York: Berkley, 1995. Paperback.

A psychopathic serial killer is on the loose in Washington, D.C. He is called the Winter Man by investigators because he strikes during snow storms. His method of execution is extremely cruel and very precise. The narrator of this page-turning detective story is vampire and forensic hematologist Nicki Chim. She refers to herself and others of her ilk as hematomans. Nicki is tough, smart, and funny. She also has a private life that is causing her no end of trouble. Her lover, Gale, is going through a difficult time. He wants to leave and start his own clan. Nicki does not know how to stop him or even if she should.

Element(s): Mystery.

257. **Wartell, Matt.** *Blood of Our Children.* Westminster, CO: Web Publishing, 1996. Paperback.

This is a most unusual vampire story, one set in the eighteenth-century Jewish ghetto of Lidz, Poland. A vampire stalks young boys and kills them just before their Bar Mitzvah. The local ruler, Count Vronski, a Catholic, and Shimon Zi, a Jewish holy man (*Tzaddick*) and scholar, work together to defeat the nosferatu. This story encompasses a rich description of European Jewish life of two hundred years ago.

Element(s): Religion.

258. **Weinberg, Robert.** Series: Masquerade of the Red Death Trilogy.
Publisher series: World of Darkness: Vampire.

The plot of this trilogy is quite complex, but it helps that the prologue to volume one (*Blood War*) has an excellent introduction to the
World of Darkness scenario. A history of the vampires, known as Kindred, is revealed by the Vatican's Father Naples, a member of the Society of Leopold, through a conversation with Reuben, a mysterious
young man who, when this conversation is finished, manages to silence
all witnesses—including Father Naples.

The Kindred are descendents of the biblical Cain and sometimes
refer to themselves as Cainites. The Kindred of modern times are divided into thirteen clans and live by rules of the Masquerade which pro-
tects the anonymity of the vampire community. Over the several thousands of years that the Kindred have existed, the clans have planned and
plotted against one another. Even within each clan members are often
literally at each other's throats. One way for a vampire to assume more
power is by killing a Kindred of an earlier generation and drinking that
victim's blood. The Kindred are a fractious lot, and into the middle of
this steps an entity who calls himself the Red Death. His body is made
of fire and everyone he touches—Kindred, Ghoul (human servants of
the vampires), or Kine (mortals)—is burned to ashes. He materializes in
various places all over the world within a short span of days. Vampire
leaders try to discern what this entity could be. None have ever seen his
like before. Two mortals become special targets of the Red Death, but
these two are more than what they seem. The first, Dire McCann, who
works for the vampire Prince of St. Louis, knows from his first brief encounter with the Red Death that it is Kindred. He uses his unique mental powers to probe the being and discovers this bit of information just
before it strikes back and almost kills him. The second mortal is the fab-
ulously wealthy Alicia Varney who lives in New York and has her own
close encounter when she attends a meeting of powerful local Kindred.
She is saved by Reuben, who seems immune to the Red Death's fiery
powers.

Eventually, the reader discovers that Dire and Alicia are the
avatars of centuries-old vampires who have found a way to walk in daylight and live as normal mortals. The Red Death has a special interest
in them as well as another known as Phantomas. This vampire lives in
underground caverns of Paris and has accumulated an intricate history
and family tree of the Kindred which he keeps on a computer.

There are many more secrets and mysteries that surround the Red

Death and his purpose. In the midst of the havoc he wreaks, the clans' bloody warfare escalates. This trilogy has a twisted, adventurous, and often violent plot.

259. ———. *Blood War*. Clarkston, GA: White Wolf, 1995. Paperback.
Series: Masquerade of the Red Death Trilogy No. 1.
Publisher series: World of Darkness: Vampire.
The Red Death appears in places where Kindred clans gather and destroys anything in its path. It also sets a trap for Dire McCann and Alicia Varney. Fortunately they have considerable powers of their own plus some help from a strange assortment of allies.

260. ———. *Unholy Allies*. Clarkston, GA: White Wolf, 1995. Paperback.
Series: Masquerade of the Red Death Trilogy No. 2.
Publisher series: World of Darkness: Vampire.
McCann learns that the Red Death has gained its terrible powers from an alliance with demonic fire spirits who once inhabited our world. Their association with the Red Death is strengthening them and may allow them to return.

261. ———. *The Unbeholden*. Clarkston, GA: White Wolf, 1996. Paperback.
Series: Masquerade of the Red Death Trilogy No. 3.
Publisher series: World of Darkness: Vampire.
McCann and Varney find out about the existence of a Kindred named Phantomas who has discovered important information about the Red Death.

262. Whalen, Patrick.
Although the following two books make up one whole story they can be read separately and enjoyed on their own terms. In each there is lots of action and adventure interspersed with some very funny scenes.

263. ———. *Monastery*. New York: Pocket Books, 1988. Paperback.
Series: Monastery No. 1.
On Chinook, an island off the coast of Washington state, a monastery is built to entomb the last remaining vampires, a group of immortals called the Ancients. When some college students break into the

vault the Ancients escape. Their leader, Gregory, wants to make the island a kingdom. He and the others begin their takeover by creating New Ones—vampires whose thirst overwhelms any remnants of their humanity. One group of humans led by Braille, a former Green Beret, holds the vampires at bay. Gregory and Braille, although adversaries, develop a grudging respect for one another.

264. ———. *Night Thirst*. New York: Pocket Books, 1991. Paperback. Series: Monastery No. 2.

Sequel to *Monastery*. After a nuclear plant explodes on Chinook Island a few vampires and humans survive. Braille is one of the survivors. He was, however, infected by a vampire bite in a fight with Gregory. Now Braille is a prisoner of Dr. Hargrave Cutter, a sadistic physician working for a rogue government agency, the Office of Strategic Medical Studies (OSMS). Cutter hopes that by studying Braille he will learn the secret of immortality. While Gregory and his fellow prisoners plot escape, another survivor of Chinook, the vampire Gregory, makes his way to a small town in Washington. When Cutter discovers Gregory's presence he sends a group of tough bounty hunters after him. The plot thickens yet again when an outbreak of murderous New Ones in Seattle claims the attention of both Braille and Gregory.

265. **Wright, T. Lucien.** *Thirst of the Vampire*. New York: Pinnacle, 1992. Paperback.

During the French Revolution Jean Paul Marat had sent many to the guillotine and in time turned on his cohort Phillippe Brissot, who fled before Marat could have him arrested. In the cave where Brissot hid he encountered a creature that turned him into a vampire. Now in modern-day America, Marat's descendents are being stalked by Brissot, who still carries a 200-year-old grudge. The Marat family finds an ally in an unexpected source.

266. **Yarbro, Chelsea Quinn.** Saint-Germain series.

Yarbro's vampire hero, Count Saint-Germain, is an alchemist and apothecary with a lifespan of more than 3,500 years. The various novels in which he is the protagonist refer to some of those ancient times. For the most part, however, the stories thus far written occur during the Common Era. Saint-German is a vampire who needs blood as nourishment, carries his native soil with him (even places bits of it in his shoes), casts no reflection, and heals from wounds that would destroy a mortal.

However, he never kills his victims, preferring to take only as much blood as he needs from a willing lover or from a stranger who knows only pleasant dreams as a result. More than just a nice guy, Saint-Germain strives to do good and to help wherever he can. Multilingual, intelligent, and rich, Saint-Germain always manages to charm his way into the most influential circles of the period. He helps people in distress and is ready to lend a hand, especially if the person is female.

Yarbro's novels always offer rich historical settings. These books are as much historical novels as vampire stories. Much background information is given through letters, sometimes from minor characters, but also between Saint-Germain and his dear friend and fellow vampire Atta Olivia Clemens.

267. ———. *Hotel Transylvania*. New York: St. Martin's, 1978. Hardcover. (Paperback. New York: Signet, 1979.)
   Series: Saint-Germain No. 1.
   The first of the Saint-Germain novels takes place in mid-eighteenth-century Paris. The object of the count's love is Madelaine de Montalia, whom he rescues from a satanic cult. In rescuing her he makes her into a vampire.
   Element(s): History, Romance.

268. ———. *The Palace*. New York: St. Martin's, 1978. Hardcover. (New York: Tor, 1988. Paperback.)
   Series: Saint-Germain No. 2.
   Renaissance-era Florence has come under the crushing influence of the fanatic monk Savonarola. Many die at the stake and Saint-Germain is himself in danger. Still, being a person of conscience, he helps others when he can. At the risk of his own life he rescues the beautiful Demitrice, former mistress of Lorenzo the Magnificent, after she is arrested and tortured by followers of the mad monk.
   Element(s): History, Romance.

269. ———. *Blood Games*. New York: St. Martin's, 1979. Hardcover. (New York: Signet, 1980. Paperback.)
   Series: Saint-Germain No. 3.
   The setting is ancient Rome under Nero's brutal rule. Our immortal hero meets and falls in love with Atta Olivia Clemens, young wife of the sadistic Senator Justus Silius. Although Saint-Germain's love eventually saves Olivia from her husband's brutality, the manner of

lovemaking they share leads to her change. Upon her death, she will rise as a vampire, and have her own series of books. (*See* #277–280.)

Element(s): History, Romance.

270. ———. *Path of the Eclipse*. New York: St. Martin's, 1981. Hardcover. (New York: Signet, 1981. Paperback) and (New York: Tor, 1988. Paperback.)

Series: Saint-Germain No. 4.

In the early part of the thirteenth century the Mongols, under Genghis Khan, are making their way throughout Asia. Saint-Germain is caught in these momentous events as he travels through China and India.

Element(s): History, Romance.

271. ———. *Tempting Fate*. New York: St. Martin's, 1982. Hardcover. (New York: Signet, 1982. Paperback.)

Series: Saint-Germain No. 5.

Saint-Germain has become the guardian of Laisha, an orphaned Russian emigré. They face the menace of the rising power of Nazism. The setting is Europe between the world wars. Madelaine also plays a prominent role in this story.

Element(s): History, Romance.

272. ———. *Darker Jewels*. New York: Tor, 1993. Hardcover.

Series: Saint-Germain No. 7.

The setting is the sixteenth-century Russia of Ivan the Terrible, close to the end of this mad monarch's reign. Count Saint-Germain is at court representing the Polish king. Here he is befriended by Boris Gudonov, who does what he can to protect our vampire hero from court intrigues. In this story the count marries, at Ivan's insistence, Xenya Koshkina, a young woman unfairly shunned by many of the nobility. Frightened of him at first, Xenya eventually comes to love her husband deeply.

Element(s): History, Romance.

273. ———. *Better in the Dark*. New York: Tor, 1993. Hardcover. (Paperback. New York: Tor, 1995.)

Series: Saint-Germain No. 8.

The setting is Saxony in the year 937 C.E. Life was harsh during Europe's Dark Ages and especially so for women. A few women through luck and force of personality surmount the barriers of their gender and obtain positions of power. The heroine, Ranegonda, is such a woman. She rules the land of Leosan for her brother, who has taken holy vows. Saint-Germain's ship has been destroyed in a storm and his body washed ashore. When found by Ranegonda, he is close to true death.

Element(s): History, Romance.

274. ———. *Mansions of Darkness*. New York: Tor, 1996. Hardcover. Series: Saint-Germain No. 9.

Saint-Germain arrives in Cuzco, Peru, not long after the conquest of the Incas by the Spanish. There he meets Acanna Tupac, a descendent of Inca nobility, a handsome woman of middle years. Although the Incas are defeated, certain Spaniards assume that great imperial treasures remain hidden. Acanna is threatened with torture unless she divulges this secret location. Saint-Germain loves her and gives her as much protection as he can.

Element(s): History, Romance.

275. ———. *Writ in Blood*. New York: Tor, 1997. Hardcover. Series: Saint-Germain No. 10.

In the years preceding the First World War, complex political and ethnic issues make Europe a tinderbox. To alleviate tension, Czar Nicholas II of Russia sends a trusted foreigner, Saint-Germain, on a mission of peace to his uncle Edward VII of Britain and his cousin Kaiser Wilhelm II of Prussia and Germany. Spies are everywhere, including the infamous British agent Sidney Reilly, who watches Saint-Germain's movements. The vampire count's life becomes even more complicated when he falls in love with artist and feminist Rowena Saxon.

Element(s): History, Romance.

276. ———. *Out of the House of Life*. New York: Tor, 1990. Hardcover. (New York: Tor, 1994. Paperback.)
Series: Madelaine de Montalia No. 1.

There are two parallel stories in this novel. The first deals with Saint-Germain's early life in Pharaonic Egypt, where he was known as Sanh-kheran. The second follows Madelaine on an archeological expedition where she tries to find the ancient site of the House of Life where Saint-Germain once toiled.

Element(s): History, Romance.

277. ————. Series: Atta Olivia Clemens. Atta Olivia Clemens is a
      woman loved by Saint Germain and turned into a vampire by
      him. They meet in *Blood Games* (*see* #269) and remain friends
      across the centuries. Olivia has her own series of adventures in
      the following books.

278. ————. *A Flame in Byzantium*. New York: Tor, 1987. Hardcover.
      Series: Atta Olivia Clemens No. 1.
      This story takes place in Constantinople during the early years of
the Byzantine Empire. Rome's grandeur is gone, and war is a constant
state of affairs. It is no longer a safe place for anyone, let alone a female
vampire. Olivia flees to Byzantium, which offers its own special dangers.
      Element(s): History, Romance.

279. ————. *Crusader's Torch*. New York: Tor, 1988. Hardcover. (Pa-
      perback. New York: Tor, 1989.)
      Series: Atta Olivia Clemens No. 2.
      Olivia resides in Tyre in the year 1189. Fearing the invasion of Is-
lamic forces, Olivia flees with the aid of a young Knight Hospitaler. The
destination is Rome, but the journey there is a perilous one.
      Element(s): History, Romance.

280. ————. *A Candle for D'Artagnan*. New York: Tor, 1989. Hard-
      cover. (Paperback. New York: St. Martin's, 1994.)
      Series: Atta Olivia Clemens No. 3.
      Once again Olivia must leave her beloved Rome. This time she
heads for France and there meets and falls in love with the Musketeer
Charles d'Artagnan.
      Element(s): History, Romance.

ANTHOLOGIES AND NOVELLAS

A note on the anthologies: For each anthology there will be a brief general statement about the collection plus annotations for a representative sampling of stories. It is often difficult to summarize a short story without giving too much away so some of the annotations may seem a bit terse. All story titles in the anthologies are listed. You will note that some stories are found in more than one collection.

281. **Brandewyne, Rebecca.** "Devil's Keep." In *Avon Books Presents Bewitching Love Stories*. New York: Avon, 1992.
   In 1813 Lenore Blakeley accepts the job of governess at an isolated manor in Cornwall, England. Her employer is a Prussian, Count Drogo von Reicher, who has come to this place with his seven-year-old son, Nikolaus. When Lenore first sees Drogo, she is captivated by his wicked good looks. What she does not realize is that he is a vampire, and that he and Nikolaus desperately need her help.

282. **Brite, Poppy Z. (editor).** *Love in Vein: Twenty Original Tales of Vampiric Erotica.* New York: HarperPrism, 1994.
   Brite, a noted horror author, has assembled a group of short stories where the erotic allure of the vampire (whether of the blood-drinking variety or imbiber of some other vital substance) is showcased.

   283. **Baker, Mike.** "Love Me Forever."

   284. **Clegg, Douglas.** "White Chapel."

   285. **de Lint, Charles.** "In This Soul of a Woman."

   286. **Devereaux, Robert.** "A Slow Red Whisper of Sand."

287. **Engstrom, Elizabeth.** "Elixir."

288. **Faust, Christa.** "Cherry."
     A young male prostitute has had fantasies about the vampire life ever since he read *Dracula*. Then one night he meets a "trick" who might just be able to make his dream come true.

289. **Hodge, Brian.** "The Alchemy of the Throat."

290. **Holder, Nancy.** "Cafe Endless: Spring Rain."

291. **Koja, Kathe, and Barry N. Malzberg.** "In the Greenhouse."

292. **McDowell, Ian.** "Geraldine."

293. **Monteleone, Thomas F.** "Triptych di Amore."

294. **Morlan, A. R.** "—And the Horses Hiss at Midnight."

295. **Partridge, Norman.** "Do Not Hasten to Bid Me Adieu."
     Everyone believes Quincey Morris died while stalking Dracula, but in this story he not only survives but has now returned to his native Texas. He dresses completely in black and hauls around an old coffin. Without giving too much away, let's just say that this is a very romantic love story, although not truly an erotic one.

296. **Pugmire, Wilum H.** "Delicious Antique Whore."

297. **Sallee, Wayne Allen.** "From Hunger."

298. **Salmonson, Jessica Amanda.** "The Final Fête of Abba Adi."
     A weird poetic tale of identical female triplets, women of such beauty that men go into ecstasy at the sight of them. One, Ernesta, marries the charismatic Abba Adi, who has a party, a fête. The guests are astonished to see a ritual sacrifice.

299. **Silva, David B.** "Empty Vessels."

300. **Tem, Melanie, and Steve Rasnic Tem.** "The Marriage."

301. **Willis, Danielle.** "The Gift of Neptune."

302. **Wolfe, Gene.** "Queen of the Night."

303. **Brownworth, Victoria A. (editor).** *Night Bites: Vampire Stories by Women.* Seattle, WA: Seal Press, 1996. Paperback.
Editor Victoria Brownworth has assembled a collection of stories whose female authors give a feminist slant to the vampire theme. Many of the tales offer something unique to those who enjoy offbeat literature.

304. **Baird, Meredith Suzanne.** "They Have No Faces."
Lovely descriptive passages grace the story of a woman who hopes to save her failing marriage by vacationing with her husband in Romania, Dracula's mythical homeland. While there she meets a handsome guide who claims to know the real people of the night.

305. **Baker, Nikki.** "Backlash."

306. **Brown, Toni.** "Immunity."

307. **Brownworth, Victoria A.** "Twelfth Night."

308. **Carr, Jan.** "Apologia."

309. **Dahme, Joanne.** "The Vampire's Baby."

310. **de la Peña, Terri.** "Refugio."

311. **DeKelb-Rittenhouse, Diane.** "To Die For."
In this highly charged erotic tale a killer is on the loose, but young Genevra is unafraid. She goes out looking for a good time and finds it. More than one vampire lurks in this story.

312. **Katz, Judith.** "Anita, Polish Vampire, Holds Forth at the Jewish Cafe of the Dead."
Miss Sadowsky seeks to interview the legendary vampire Anita Lepski. The lady gets her wish in this witty little story with a lesbian twist.

313. **Maney, Mabel.** "Almost the Color of Summer Sky."

314. **Redding, Judith M.** "Unexpurgated Notes from a Homicide Case File."

315. **Robson, Ruthann.** "Women's Music."

316. **Sturgis, Susanna J.** "Sustenance."

317. **Wagner, Joyce.** "Bad Company."

318. **Williamson, Lisa D.** "Best of Friends."

319. **Wright, Linda K.** "The Last Train."

320. **Dozois, Gardner, and Sheila Williams (editors).** *Isaac Asimov's Vampires.* New York: Ace, 1996.
This is a collection of eight vampire stories that appeared in the pages of the magazine *Asimov's Science Fiction.*

321. **Cadigan, Pat.** "My Brother's Keeper."
A young woman named China enters the underworld of junkies and addicts in an attempt to locate her brother Joe. She finds him, eventually, but she also discovers a world of vampires that prey on those beaten down by drugs.

322. **Farber, Sharon N.** "A Surfeit of Melancholic Humours."
In London of 1665 a terrible plague kills thousands of people. The devastation is so terrible that the young physician and narrator of this tale, Dr. William Praisegood, fears the city will soon become a mausoleum. Then he meets a foreigner, a pale-faced gentleman with a penchant for drinking blood, who seems completely immune to the plague. (*See* #8 where Dr. Praisegood also appears as a character.)

323. **Frost, Gregory.** "Some Things Are Better Left."

324. **Lee, Tanith.** "Winter Flowers."

325. **Palwick, Susan.** "Ever After."

326. **Redd, David.** "The Old Man of Munington."
Jenny is nine years old and quite prescient when in the presence

of supernatural beings like Claude Munington (the Old Man). She figures out he is a vampire, but only the reader knows that he is one of a race of guardians for humanity. The tale is set in 1950s Wales.

327. **Tiedmann, Mark W.** "Drink."

328. **Willis, Connie.** "Jack."

329. **Drake, Shannon.** "Vanquish the Night." In *Avon Presents Bewitching Love Stories*. New York: Avon, 1992.
Anne Pemberton loves Michael Johnston but refuses to marry him. In West Texas the truce with the Apaches is a tenuous one, and Michael, as head of the militia, has a dangerous job. Anne lost a husband in the Civil War. She does not want to lose another. Into town one night comes David Drago, a man who mesmerizes women when he is not out murdering for blood. He is a vampire who decides he wants Anne to share his life. If she is to survive, Michael must fight for her.

330. **Elrod, P. N., and Martin H. Greenberg (editors).** *The Time of the Vampires*. New York: Daw, 1996. Paperback.
This collection of eighteen original stories tells of vampires throughout various periods of history beginning with ancient Greece and Rome and ending at the present. Authors' notes follow each story, giving brief historical background or telling something of particular interest about the setting.

331. **Barrett, Julie.** "Night of the Vampire Scare."

332. **Bergstrom, Elaine.** "The Ghost of St. Mark's."
In her novel *Shattered Glass* (*see* #15) Bergstrom mentions the death of David Austra during World War II. This is the beautifully told story of his final days and his final release.

333. **Booth, Susan.** "Scent of Blood."

334. **Brothers, Rebecca Ann.** "Death Mask."

335. **Carl, Lillian Stewart.** "The Blood of the Lamb."

336. **Carter, Margaret L.** "Voice from the Void."

In this light romantic tale, the vampire Claude D'Arnot has joined a group devoted to the supernatural. He has discovered that the women in this group mlake easy prey for his special needs. Now Claude has his eye on Violet, but she has preternatural talents that surprise even this worldly undead. The setting is late eighteenth-century England.

337. **Elrod, P. N.** "The Devil's Mark."
In seventeenth-century England a witch hunter enters a small village, relishing the idea of a nice witch-burning. Unfortunately for him, the inhabitants are a far cry from the easily led country bumpkins he thought them to be.

338. **Graham, Jean.** "Walking Tour."

339. **Huff, Tanya.** "What Manner of Man."
The hero of this tale is Henry Fitzroy, the vampire who is a friend of Vicki Nelson in Huff's modern-day mystery series (*see* #126–131). The setting is Regency England (1811–1820). One night Henry rescues an aristocratic gentleman who has been attacked and almost killed. This incident propels Henry into a game of intrigue where French spies are trying to wrest British secrets in order to help Napoleon.

340. **Kilpatrick, Nancy.** "In Memory Of."
This story suggests an interesting twist on what may have been behind the inspiration of Bram Stoker's Dracula. It was not Vlad Tepes, but Oscar Wilde's vampiric seduction of Florence Balcombe a few years before she married Bram.

341. **Kingsgrave-Ernstein, Catt.** "Bloodthirsty Tyrants."

342. **Longstreet, Roxanne.** "Faith Like Wine."

343. **Patterson, Teresa.** "The Gift."

344. **Pollotta, Nick.** "A Matter of Taste."

345. **Schimel, Lawrence.** "Black Sounds."
In early twentieth-century Spain, a man desperately craves the gypsy/flamenco world of poetry and music. But the essence of its vi-

brancy eludes his soul. Then a beautiful woman seemingly offers exactly what he seeks.

346. **Schutte, James.** "Toothless Vampires Can Still Give Hickeys."

347. **Sinor, Bradley H.** "Oaths."
The vampire in this tale once had the name Sir Lancelot. Now centuries later, during Europe's Middle Ages, he is reminded of an oath he swore to King Arthur. It is very much like the one he swore when he became a Templar. He is a man of his word.

348. **Tilton, Lois.** "A Vision of Darkness."
The setting is ancient Greece. Socrates meets a ghostly being who tells him what it is truly like to die. But this shade has substance and thrives on human blood.

349. **Greenberg, Martin H. (editor).** *Vampire Detectives.* New York: Daw, 1995.
In this collection of nineteen original stories, we encounter vampires who are detectives as well as detectives who hunt vampires.

350. **Borton, Douglas.** "Fangs."

351. **Collins, Max Allan.** "The Night of Their Lives."

352. **Crowther, Peter.** "Home Comforts."

353. **Elrod, P. N.** "You'll Catch Your Death."
A Jack Fleming story (*see* #65–71 for novels based on this character). This time Jack runs into a frightened lady while walking along Chicago's lake shore. He offers his help only to find himself in deep trouble.

354. **Hoch, Edward D.** "No Blood for a Vampire."

355. **Holder, Nancy.** "Undercover."

356. **Huff, Tanya.** "This Town Ain't Big Enough."
A Vicki Nelson story (*see* #126–131 for novels based on this character). Vicki gives some unwanted help to her detective friend

Mike. There has been a murder and Vicki's new paranormal senses tell her that the killer is a vampire.

357. **Ketchum, Jack.** "The Turning."

358. **Kisner, James.** "God-Less Men."

359. **Koja, Kathe, and Barry N. Malzberg.** "Girl's Night Out."

360. **Laymon, Richard.** "Phil the Vampire."

361. **Lutz, John.** "Shell Game."

362. **Maclay, John.** "Tom Rudolph's Last Tape."

363. **Nolan, William F.** "Vampire Dollars."

364. **Paul, Barbara.** "The Secret."

365. **Ruse, Gary Alan.** "Night Tidings."

366. **Sallee, Wayne Allen.** "Blind Pig on North Halsted."

367. **Sanders, William.** "The Count's Mailbox."

368. **Williamson, J. N.** "Origin of a Species."
    Archaeology is the hobby and passion of police detective Erwin Parrish. The finding of a perfectly preserved, several-thousand-year-old body on Mount Ararat attracts his attention and allows him to put his investigative skills to work on a terrifying mystery.

369. **Greenberg, Martin H. (editor).** *Celebrity Vampires.* New York: Daw, 1995. Paperback.
    The title says it all. Each story revolves around some famous person and his or her encounter with the vampire world. This book contains nineteen original stories.

370. **Baker, Mike.** "The Swashbuckler and the Vampire."

371. **Braunbeck, Gary A.** "Bloody Sam."

372. **Breen, Jon L.** "Woollcott and the Vamp."

373. **Collins, Barbara.** "Sweet Dreams, Norma Jean."
While living in Manhattan, Marilyn Monroe's kind gesture to an injured bat earns her the undying devotion of a vampire.

374. **Collins, Max Allan.** "Traces of Red."

375. **Crider, Bill.** "King of the Night."

376. **Crowther, Peter.** "Too Short a Death."

377. **D'Amato, Barb.** "I Vant to Be Alone."

378. **Douglas, Carole Nelson.** "Dracula on the Rocks."

379. **Elrod, P. N.** "A Night at the (Horse) Opera."

380. **Haber, Karen.** "The Vampire of the Opera."

381. **Knight, Tracy A.** "Blessed by His Dying Tongue."
The various Elvis sightings may be true after all. In this story the King feels exhausted. He needs a break to recharge his batteries before making a comeback. A fan who is also a vampire has just the remedy: Elvis must join the ranks of the undead.

382. **Lee, Wendi, and Terry Beatty.** "Death on the Mississippi."

383. **Lutz, John.** "Plague."

384. **Partridge, Norman.** "Undead Origami."

385. **Paul, Barbara.** "Totally Tallulah."

386. **Ranieri, Roman A.** "A Singular Event on a Night in 1912."

387. **Rusch, Kristine Kathryn.** "The Beautiful, The Damned."

388. **Williamson, J. N.** "Vladimir's Conversions."
The course of the Russian Revolution and the fate of the royal

family greatly depended on the special relationship of a vampire, Grigori Rasputin, and his mortal ally, Vladimir Lenin, leader of the Bolshevik Party.

389. **Hambly, Barbara, and Martin H. Greenberg (editors).** *Sisters of the Night.* New York: Warner Books, 1995.
    This collage of fourteen short stories centers on the female vampire. Themes range from eerie and despairing to humorous.

390. **Cadigan, Pat.** "Sometimes Salvation."

391. **Effinger, George Alec.** "Marîd and the Trail of Blood."

392. **Hambly, Barbara.** "Madeleine."
    In this darkly humorous tale, an amoral vampire, Madeleine, is driven crazy by a curse from a mortal. Now whenever Madeleine drinks her victims' blood, their thoughts play over and over in her mind.

393. **Harrison, M. John.** "Empty."

394. **Hoffman, Nina Kiriki.** "Food Chain."

395. **Kurland, Michael.** "In the Blood."
    Adolescence is always difficult but especially so for young vampire Almeric, who must come to terms with what he is.

396. **Lee, Tanith.** "La Dame."

397. **Niven, Larry.** "Song of the Night People."
    This novella makes up the first four chapters of Niven's science fiction novel *The Ringworld Throne.*

398. **Paxson, Diana L.** "The Bloodbeast."

399. **Rusch, Kristine Kathryn.** "Victims."
    The vampire Veronique becomes embroiled in a modern-day political campaign

400. **Smith, Dean Wesley.** "Tumbling Down the Nighttime."
    An old man in a nursing home prays for death, and then his

long-lost love pays him a visit. She has not changed a bit in forty years. She offers to grant his wish.

401. **Tem, Melanie, and Steve Tem.** "Mama."
Elizabeth's dead mother is back. A nightmarish tale of a mother's consuming love.

402. **Wheeler, Deborah.** "Survival Skills."
In this comic story a truant officer tells Valeria, a vampire single mom, that she must send her children to school. Luckily, there is a special school just for kids of parents who work at night.

403. **Yolen, Jane.** "Sister Death."

404. **Jones, Stephen (editor).** *The Mammoth Book of Vampires.* New York: Carroll & Graf, 1992.
A collection of short stories, novellas and one poem from modern masters of horror such as Clive Barker, Ramsey Campbell and Brian Lumley as well as classic writers like Edgar Allan Poe, M. R. James, E. F. Benson and, of course, Bram Stoker.

405. **Barker, Clive.** "Human Remains."

406. **Benson, E. F.** "The Room in the Tower."

407. **Bloch, Robert.** "Hungarian Rhapsody."
Retired gangster Solly Vincent is intrigued by his new neighbor, a gorgeous lady from Hungary, only seen at night, and who pays for her property with gold coins from the reign of Emperor Franz Joseph.

408. **Campbell, Ramsey.** "The Brood."

409. **Cave, Hugh B.** "Stragella."
Two men are adrift at sea for days and think their ordeal is over when they see a large ship approaching through the fog. Unfortunately, their journey of horror has only begun.

410. **Chetwynd-Hayes, R.** "The Labyrinth."
A young couple, lost on the English moors, find out what horror occurs when a vampire is staked and buried but does not die.

411. **Copper, Basil.** "Doctor Porthos."

412. **Crawford, F. Marion.** "For the Blood Is the Life."
Originally published in 1911 as part of a collection entitled *Wandering Ghosts*. On moonlit nights an unmarked grave shows the shimmering outline of a body lying on top of it. This marks the grave of a vampire.

413. **Daniels, Les.** "Yellow Fog."
A novel (*see* #54 for annotation).

414. **Etchison, Dennis.** "It Comes out Only at Night."

415. **Gaiman, Neil.** "Vampire Sestina."

416. **Garfield, Frances.** "The House at Evening."
Two young men enter an old victorian house with two beautiful women who, they are assured, can provide an evening's entertainment. The ladies, however, are almost as old as the house and have very sharp canines.

417. **Holder, Nancy.** "Blood Gothic."

418. **James, M. R.** "An Episode of Cathedral History."

419. **Lumley, Brian.** "Necros."

420. **Masterton, Graham.** "Laird of Dunain."

421. **Matheson, Richard Christian.** "Vampire."

422. **Newman, Kim.** "Red Reign."
This novella was written before the novel *Anno-Dracula* (*see* #191) and is actually an alternate telling of the story.

423. **Poe, Edgar Allan.** "Ligeia."

424. **Schow, David J.** "A Week in the Unlife."

425. **Stableford, Brian N.** "The Man Who Loved the Vampire Lady."

This story is the opening chapter of Stableford's novel *The Empire of Fear* (*see* entry #242).

426. **Stoker, Bram.** "Dracula's Guest."
This story was originally written as a chapter in the novel *Dracula* (*see* #245), but did not make the final cut. Here Jonathan Harker encounters another vampire from whom he is protected by the Count.

427. **Tem, Melanie.** "The Better Half."

428. **Tem, Steve Rasnic.** "Vintage Domestic."

429. **Tremayne, Peter.** "Dracula's Chair."

430. **Wagner, Karl Edward.** "Beyond Any Measure."
Terrifying images of blood and death invade the dreams and waking hours of a young woman. She even has visions of a vampiric doppelganger.

431. **Waldrop, Howard.** "Der Untergang Des Abendlandesmenschen."

432. **Wellman, Manly Wade.** "Chastel."

433. **Wilson, F. Paul.** "Midnight Mass."

434. **Jones, Stephen (editor).** *The Mammoth Book of Dracula.* New York: Carroll & Graf, 1997. Paperback.
Stephen Jones bids us welcome in this collection of Dracula-centered stories which, when read in sequence, produce a fictionalized history of literature's most enduring vampire. There is a mixture of original stories and reprints including the prologue of a dramatic reading of Stoker's *Dracula.* The foreword comes from Daniel Farson, Stoker's biographer and great-nephew. The story titles listed below are in order as they appear in the anthology.

435. **Stoker, Bram.** "Dracula: or The Un-Dead: Prologue."
On May 18, 1897, a few weeks before the publication of *Dracula* (*see* #245), Stoker produced a single-performance play based on his novel. With minor corrections, this is the prologue for that play as presented at London's Royal Lyceum Theatre.

436. **Fowler, Christopher.** "Dracula's Library."

437. **Ligotti, Thomas.** "The Heart of Count Dracula, Descendant of Attila, Scourge of God."

438. **Slater, Mandy.** "Daddy's Little Girl."

439. **Campbell, Ramsey.** "Conversion."

440. **Wellman, Manly Wade.** "The Devil Is Not Mocked."

441. **Kilpatrick, Nancy.** "Teaserama."
It's been a while since Vlad has had that love-struck feeling, but he has it now. He is completely smitten with a lovely, lithesome actress who stars in porn flicks.

442. **Holder, Nancy.** "Blood Freak."

443. **Lumley, Brian.** "Zack Phalanx is Vlad the Impaler."

444. **Copper, Basil.** "When Greek Meets Greek."

445. **Newman, Kim.** "Coppola's Dracula."
If Francis Ford Coppola had invested the same intensity and encountered the same problems in the making of *Dracula* as he did in *Apocalypse Now*, the resultant movie-making experience might have been very much as described in this short story. Months behind schedule, way over budget, and filming on location in Communist-controlled Romania, Coppola spends endless hours screaming at the crew and rewriting scenes. No one knows how the story will end. After two weeks of work, Harvey Keitel is fired and Martin Sheen takes over the part of Jonathan Harker. Marlon Brando signs on at the last minute to play Dracula. The setting is the same bizarre, alternate world Newman created for *Anno Dracula* and *The Bloody Red Baron* (*see* #191–192).

446. **Cave, Hugh B.** "The Second Time Around."

447. **Mooney, Brian.** "Endangered Species."

448. **Lannes, Roberta.** "Melancholia."

449. **Morton, Lisa.** "Children of the Long Night."

450. **Royle, Nicholas.** "Mbo."

451. **McAuley, Paul J.** "The Worst Place in the World."

452. **Smith, Guy N.** "Larry's Guest."

453. **Edwards, Jan.** "A Taste of Culture."

454. **Chetwynd-Hayes, R.** "Rudolph."

455. **Masterton, Graham.** "Roadkill."

456. **Lamsley, Terry.** "Volunteers."

457. **Gordon, John.** "Black Beads."

458. **Lane, Joel.** "Your European Son."

459. **Stableford, Brian.** "Quality Control."

460. **Smith, Michael Marshall.** "Dear Alison."

461. **Williams, Conrad.** "Bloodlines."

462. **Morgan, Chris.** "Windows '99 of the Soul."
In the late twentieth century, Dracula has found a new way to exist and survive in a world dominated by computers.

463. **Chinn, Mike.** "Blood of Eden."

464. **Hodge, Brian.** "The Last Testament."

465. **Crowther, Peter.** "The Last Vampire."

466. **Wilson, F. Paul.** "The Lord's Work."

467. **Fletcher, Jo.** "Lord of the Undead."

468. **Keesey, Pam (editor).** *Daughters of Darkness: Lesbian Vampire Stories.* Pittsburgh, PA: Cleis Press, 1993. Hardcover and paperback.

An erudite introduction by Pam Keesey gives a history of the lesbian vampire in myth, fiction, and film. Careful attention is paid to Le Fanu's *Carmilla* and its continuing influence. She also discusses the importance of the historical Elizabeth Bathory on Bram Stoker's *Dracula*. The themes of each story in the collection are vampiric, though not always the traditional bloodsucking variety. A filmography of lesbian vampire movies is included.

469. **Bergstrom, Elaine.** "Daughter of the Night."
Excerpt from the novel (*see* #18).

470. **Califia, Pat.** "The Vampire."

471. **Forrest, Katherine V.** "O Captain, My Captain."

472. **Gomez, Jewelle.** "Louisiana: 1850."
Excerpt from *The Gilda Stories* (*see* #97).

473. **LeFanu, J. Sheridan.** "Carmilla."

474. **Livia, Anna.** "Minimax."

475. **Minns, Karen Marie Christa.** "Virago."

476. **Scott, Jody.** "I, Vampire."
A girl of thirteen is thrown out of the castle when her parents learn she has inherited that defective gene that makes her a bloodsucking spawn of Satan.

477. **Sommers, Robbi.** "Lilith."

478. **zana.** "Dracula Retold."
This is a short, funny story with a modern-day lucy harker (sic) married to male chauvenist real estate agent jonathan. A new neighbor, ms. dracula, teaches lucy how to be a real woman.

479. **Keesey, Pam (editor).** *Dark Angels: Lesbian Vampire Stories.* Pittsburgh, PA: Cleis Press, 1995. Paperback.

A second collection of vampire stories with erotic lesbian themes from editor Pam Keesey. In her introduction Keesey invokes several mythic aspects of the Goddess and her relationship to vampire lore. The dark Hindu deity Kali, a bloodthirsty goddess with a necklace of skulls, is a fine example. Then there is Lilith, the seductress who according to legend was Adam's first wife, though she seemed to prefer the company of demon lovers. The introduction is at least as interesting as any of the stories.

480. **Bowen, Gary.** "Blood Wedding."

481. **Charles, Renee M.** "Cinnamon Roses."

What is it really like having to make it in the modern world as a vampire? Well, it's not easy. Drinking blood doesn't pay the rent. The newly transformed undead narrator of this story makes a living as a hairstylist in an all-night place that attracts the punk, S & M, adventurous types. The scissors and razors of her trade make it fairly easy to tap into a food supply without drawing too much attention. It's also a good place to meet a new lover.

482. **Daniels, Cora Linn.** "The Countess Visonti."

483. **Dell, Shawn.** "Daria Dangerous."

484. **G, Amelia.** "Wanting."

485. **Leonard, Carol.** "Medea."

486. **Pizarnik, Alejandra.** "The Bloody Countess."

487. **Roche, Thomas S.** "Orphans."

488. **Schimel, Lawrence.** "Femme-de-Siècle."

A comic tale in which the narrator, a self described "bulldagger," begins an intense affair with a Geena-Davis-like femme. It takes a few weeks but suddenly the narrator realizes that her new girlfriend never eats—food. She is, of course, a vampire who keeps her girlish figure by only imbibing blood from anemics.

489. **Tan, Cecilia.** "The Tale of Christina."

490. **Tem, Melanie.** "Presence."

491. **Lee, Tanith.** "Red as Blood." In *Red as Blood or Tales from the Sisters Grimmer*. New York: DAW, 1983.
This oddly spiritual story is a poetic retelling of Snow White. Here is Bianca with hair as black as night, skin as white as snow, and lips as red as blood. She looks just like her mother who died soon after Bianca's birth. The new queen suspects her stepdaughter may be responsible for a strange incurable wasting disease that plagues the land. She is right. Bianca is a vampire.

492. **McCammon, Robert R. (editor).** *Under the Fang*. New York: Pocket Books, 1991. Paperback.
The premise of all the stories in this anthology is that the world is dominated by vampires. Humans live in fear of the night. "Introduction" by editor McCammon is itself a short story and sets the tone for those that follow.

493. **McCammon, Robert R.** "Introduction."
The narrator tells of the terror suffered in a world where vampires have suddenly taken over. Some humans have banded together to fight the oppressor, but for now the power resides with the bloodsuckers.

494. **Brooks, Clifford V.** "There Are No Nightclubs in East Palo Alto."

495. **Cantrell, Lisa W.** "Juice."

496. **Charnas, Suzy McKee, and Chelsea Quinn Yarbro.** "Advocates."
Subtitled, "A Novelet Featuring Weyland (*see* #35) and Saint-Germain (*see* #266–275)." Even in a world dominated by vampires Edward Weyland is considered a monster. He thinks of vampires as well as humans as prey. The Magistrates want him executed, but Saint-Germain offers his services as Weyland's advocate.

497. **Collins, Clint.** "Stoker's Mistress."

498. **Collins, Nancy A.** "Dancing Nightly."

This dark story describes a typical night in the unlife of a vampire. Mavrides leaves his coffin at dusk, goes to a vampires-only night spot, Club Vlad, and watches human gladiators fight in cages suspended from the ceiling. This allows their blood to drip down into the waiting throats of the crowd below.

499. **de Lint, Charles.** "We Are Dead Together."

500. **Gorman, Ed.** "Duty."

501. **Hodge, Brian.** "Midnight Sun."

502. **Laymon, Richard.** "Special."

503. **McCammon, Robert R.** "The Miracle Mile."

504. **Meyer, David N. III** "A Bloodsucker."

505. **Monteleone, Thomas F.** "Prodigal Sun."

506. **Perez, Dan.** "Behind Enemy Lines."

507. **Sarrantonio, Al.** "Red Eve."

508. **Williams, Sidney, and Robert Petitt.** "Does the Blood Line Run on Time?"

509. **Williamson, Chet.** "Calm Sea and Prosperous Voyage."

510. **Williamson, J. N.** "Herrenrasse."

511. **Preiss, Byron (editor).** *The Ultimate Dracula.* New York: Dell, 1991. Paperback.
    In 1931, the motion picture *Dracula,* starring Bela Lugosi, introduced many to Stoker's infamous character. The 1991 publication of this anthology celebrates the film's sixtieth anniversary with nineteen original stories by authors such as Anne Rice, Dan Simmons, Ron Dee, and Mike Resnick. Many stories, but not all, include the Dracula character. An introduction by Leonard Wolf briefly discusses the original film and the novel. The book concludes with a selected filmography.

512. **Anderson, Kevin J.** "Much at Stake."

513. **Asimov, Janet.** "The Contagion."

514. **Betancourt, John Gregory.** "In the Cusp of the Hour."

515. **Dee, Ron.** "A Matter of Style."
Neville, undead at age twenty-six, thinks "life" will be better now that he has the powers of a vampire. Rejections by women will be a thing of the past. He studies Bela Lugosi's *Dracula* and tries to emulate the suave charm—unsuccessfully, as it turns out. Then one night he meets a woman who teaches him a very important lesson.

516. **Farmer, Philip José.** "Nobody's Perfect."

517. **Gorman, Ed.** "Selection Process."
A group of undead want to know if a certain hit man is ruthless enough to join their ranks.

518. **Graham, Heather.** "The Vampire in His Closet."

519. **Hoch, Edward D.** "Dracula 1944."

520. **Lochte, Dick.** "Vampire Dreams."

521. **Lutz, John.** "Mr. Lucrada."

522. **Philbrick, W. R.** "The Dark Rising."

523. **Resnick, Mike.** "A Little Night Music."
This is a comic look at Dracula as a rock musician. He heads a group called Vlad and the Impalers. The hip-talking Los Angeles agent who narrates the story has no idea why his new client only comes out at night, will not work on boats or in churches, and screams when a garlic pizza gets too close.

524. **Rice, Anne.** "The Master of Rampling Gate."
When Julie's father dies he exhorts her brother, Richard, to destroy the ancestral home Rampling Gate. Julie and Richard decide to visit the place (which neither has ever seen) before carrying out

their father's edict. They discover an enormous mansion where each finds a special peace and happiness. Then one night Julie meets the real master of Rampling Gate. He is a young-looking, very handsome vampire. He makes her an irresistible offer.

525. **Robards, Karen.** "Sugar and Spice and . . ."

526. **Rusch, Kristine Kathryn.** "Children of the Night."
This story forms the basis for the novel *Sins of the Blood* (*see* #212).

527. **Simmons, Dan.** "All Dracula's Children."
The setting is Romania, late December 1989, just after Ceaucescu's execution. A group of Americans arrive to witness first hand the horrors created by the late dictator's regime. Simmons describes the terrible suffering of all the people but most heartbreaking is that of the orphaned children, warehoused in filthy, unheated buildings, many in the advanced stages of AIDS. This story forms the basis for the first six chapters of *Children of the Night* (*see* #232).

528. **Sullivan, Tim.** "Los Niños de la Noche."

529. **Tem, Steve Rasnic, and Melanie Tem.** "The Tenth Scholar."
A desperate young woman, sixteen and pregnant, enters an exclusive school run by Dracula. There are ten students, and when the classes have finished, one will be invited to stay. She is sure that she will be that special one because her need for him is so great. Dracula, however, has other plans.

530. **Watt-Evans, Lawrence.** "The Name of Fear."

531. **Ryan, Alan (editor).** *Vampires: Two Centuries of Great Vampire Stories*. New York: Doubleday, 1987. Hardcover. (Paperback edition. *The Penguin Book of Vampire Stories: Two Centuries of Great Stories with a Bite*. New York: Penguin, 1988.)
This anthology contains thirty-two stories that span more than a hundred years beginning with dueling versions of *The Vampyre* by Polidori and Lord Byron and ending with a short story by the prolific fantasy writer Tanith Lee. In between are found the classic tales like Le Fanu's *Carmilla* and F. Marion Crawford's *For the Blood is the Life* and an excerpt from Rymer's infamously long novel, *Varney the Vampyre, or, The*

Feast of Blood. Also included are brief, annotated lists of vampire novels and films. As in this anthology the stories are listed in order of the date of original publication.

532. **Byron, George Gordon, Lord.** "Fragment of a Novel" (1816).

533. **Polidori, John.** "The Vampyre" (1819).

534. **Rymer, James Malcolm.** "Varney the Vampyre, or, the Feast of Blood" (1845) (excerpt).

535. **Anonymous.** "The Mysterious Stranger" (1860).

536. **LeFanu, J. Sheridan.** "Carmilla" (1872).
    Laura relates the horrifying events that surrounded her meeting with a beautiful young woman named Carmilla. At first, Carmilla seems a gracious, friendly girl, although a bit mysterious about her family. Laura thinks it only a coincidence that Carmilla resembles the portrait of the long dead Mircalla, Countess Karnstein. But it is not a coincidence. She is a most dangerous and seductive vampire.

537. **Braddon, Mary Elizabeth.** "Good Lady Ducayne" (1896).

538. **Stoker, Bram.** "Dracula's Guest" (1897).

539. **Wilkins-Freeman, Mary E.** "Luella Miller" (1903).

540. **Crawford, F. Marion.** "For the Blood Is the Life" (1911).

541. **Blackwood, Algernon.** "The Transfer" (1912).

542. **Benson, E. F.** "The Room in the Tower" (1912).

543. **James, M. R.** "An Episode of Cathedral History" (1919).

544. **Smith, Clark Ashton.** "A Rendezvous in Averoigne" (1931).

545. **Moore, C. (Catherine) L.** "Shambleau" (1933).
    Written in 1933, this classic story is based on the myth of Medusa. In a future time when Mars has been colonized, a man pro-

tects a pretty female humanoid from a mob. They call her Shambleau, but he has no idea what that means until it is almost too late. Although this is not a blood-drinking vampire story, it is annotated in this bibliography because it was one of the first to directly use the sexual themes so prominent in modern vampire fiction.

546. **Jacobi, Carl.** "Revelations in Black" (1933).

547. **Wellman, Manly Wade.** "School for the Unspeakable" (1937).

548. **Derleth, August.** "The Drifting Snow" (1939).

549. **Miller, P. Schuyler.** "Over the River" (1941).

550. **Leiber, Fritz.** "The Girl with the Hungry Eyes" (1949).

551. **Kornbluth, C. M.** "The Mindworm" (1950).

552. **Matheson, Richard.** "Drink My Blood" (1951).

553. **Beaumont, Charles.** "Place of Meeting" (1953).

554. **Bloch, Robert.** "The Living Dead" (1967).

555. **Aickman, Robert.** "Pages from a Young Girl's Journal" (1975). The nameless narrator is traveling through Italy with her parents. She speaks of her loneliness and boredom, which is finally relieved when they stop in Ravenna as guests of a countess. One night the countess gives a party, and the girl meets a wonderful man with whom she falls secretly in love. She does not worry a bit when others notice how very pale she has become and that she has strange bite marks on her neck. An interesting story with a classic vampire theme.

556. **Chetwynd-Hayes, R.** "The Werewolf and the Vampire" (1975).

557. **Grant, Charles L.** "Love-Starved" (1979).

558. **Yarbro, Chelsea Quinn.** "Cabin" (1980).

559. **Charnas, Suzy McKee.** "Unicorn Tapestry" (1980).

560. **Ryan, Alan.** "Following the Way" (1982).

561. **Campbell, Ramsey.** "The Sunshine Club" (1983).

562. **Tem, Steve Rasnic.** "The Men & Women of Rivendale" (1984).

563. **Lee, Tanith.** "Bite-Me-Not or, Fleur De Feu" (1984).

564. **Schimel, Lawrence, and Martin H. Greenberg (editors).** *Blood Lines: Vampire Stories from New England.* Nashville, TN: Cumberland House, 1997. Paperback.
Publisher series: The American Vampire.
This anthology consists of nine reprinted stories and one original (by editor Schimel). Vampires haunt New Hampshire, Massachusetts, Connecticut, Maine, Vermont, and Rhode Island in this collection.

565. **Cave, Hugh B.** "The Brotherhood of Blood."

566. **Friesner, Esther M.** "Moonlight in Vermont."
In Wintersend, Vermont, live the Harrimans, a family of vampires much loved, respected, and protected by the local citizens. Unfortunately their very existence is threatened by the spoiled son of some New York tourists. This young man knows a vampire when he sees one, and promises to stalk them one and all unless they bring him into their ranks.

567. **Lovecraft, H. P.** "The Shunned House."

568. **Pierce, Earl Jr.** "The Doom of the House of Duryea."

569. **Rusch, Kristine Kathryn.** "The Beautiful, the Damned."

570. **Schimel, Lawrence.** "Secret Societies."
A senior at Yale University has always had an unquenchable thirst for knowledge. Then one night, in the library stacks, he meets others with a similar thirst for knowledge but also one for blood.

571. **Smith, Sarah.** "When the Red Storm Comes."
Against the background of the brokered peace of the Russo-Japanese War at Portsmouth, a young woman is seduced into the power-filled vampire world.

572. **Wellman, Manly Wade.** "Chastel."

573. **Wilkins-Freeman, Mary E.** "Luella Miller."

574. **Yarbro, Chelsea Quinn.** "Investigating Jericho."

575. **Shayne, Maggie.** "Beyond Twilight." In *Strangers in the Night.* New York: Silhouette, 1995.
Series: Wings of the Night (*see* #225–229).
DPI (Division of Paranormal Investigations) agent Stephen Bachman has recurring erotic dreams about Cuyler Jade, the vampiress he hunts. Then she turns the tables and traps him. She explains that she has had the same dreams and feels a connection to him that should not exist. This should only happen between a vampire and a Chosen. He agrees to help explain this mystery, but now DPI has them both on the run.

576. **Shepard, Leslie (editor).** *The Dracula Book of Great Vampire Stories.* Secaucus, NJ: Citadel, 1977. Hardcover (Republished as Classic Vampire Stories. Secaucus, NJ: Citadel, 1995)
A collection of thirteen vampire classics including *Carmilla, For the Blood Is the Life, Dracula's Guest,* and *Mrs. Amworth.*

577. **Benson, E. F.** "Mrs. Amworth."
To the small English village of Maxley comes the lively widow Mrs. Amworth. Everyone enjoys the company of this gregarious lady except Francis Urcombe, a retired Cambridge professor who studies the occult and knows a vampire when he meets one.

578. ———. "The Room in the Tower."

579. **Blackwood, Algernon.** "The Transfer."

580. **Braddon, Mary Elizabeth.** "Good Lady Ducayne."

581. **Crawford, F. Marion.** "For the Blood Is the Life."

582. **De Maupassant, Guy.** "The Horla."

583. **Hartmann, Dr. Franz.** "An Authenticated Vampire Story."

584. **LeFanu, J. Sheridan.** "Carmilla."

585. **Loring, F. G.** "The Tomb of Sarah."

586. **Neruda, Jan.** "The Vampire."

587. **Roman, Victor.** "Four Wooden Stakes."

588. **Stenbock, Count Stanislaus Eric.** "The Sad Story of a Vampire."
    In the isolated region of Styria a young boy falls under the evil spell of the vampire Count Vardalek. The story of the boy's sad fate is narrated by his sister Carmela.

589. **Stoker, Bram.** "Dracula's Guest."

590. **Stephens, John Richard (editor).** *Vampires, Wine and Roses.* New York: Berkley, 1997. Paperback.
    Here is a collection of stories and poems from a wide ranging group of writers many of whom are not usually associated with the vampire genre—writers such as Shakespeare, Rod Serling, Sir Thomas Malory, Woody Allen, and F. Scott Fitzgerald. Although all entries have certain vampiric elements the inclusion of some stretches the limits of what is normally associated with this literature.

591. **Aiken, Conrad.** "The Divine Pilgrim" (excerpt).

592. **Allen, Woody.** "Count Dracula."
    A funny little tale wherein the Count comes out of his coffin very early one day mistaking a total eclipse of the sun for nighttime. Now the deathly rays from earth's bright star threaten to annihilate him.

593. **Baudelaire.** "The Metamorphoses of a Vampire."

594. ———. "The Vampire."

595. **Bradbury, Ray.** "The Homecoming."
    At a family gathering on Allhallows Eve, young Timothy must face the fact that he will never be like his other relatives. He hates blood, can't get used to sleeping by day, and, most embarrassingly of all, he is afraid of the dark.

596. **Bruce, Lenny.** Untitled.

597. **Byron, George Gordon, Lord.** "A Fragment of a Turkish Tale."

598. ———. "The Giaour" (excerpt).

599. **De Maupassant, Guy.** "The Horla."

600. **Doyle, Sir Arthur Conan.** "John Barrington Cowles."

601. **Dumas, Alexandre.** "The Vampire of the Carpathian Mountains."

602. **Eliot, T. S.** "The Wasteland" (excerpt).

603. **Fitzgerald, F. Scott.** "The Vampires Won't Vampire for Me."

604. **Goethe, Johann Wolfgang von.** "The Bride of Corinth."

605. **Hardy, Thomas.** "The Vampirine Fair."

606. **Keats, John.** "Lamia."

607. **Kipling, Rudyard.** "The Vampire."

608. **Lovecraft, H. P.** "The Hound."

609. **Malory, Sir Thomas.** "The Death of King Arthur" (excerpt).

610. **Poe, Edgar Allan.** "Ligeia."

611. **Rice, Anne.** "The Ballad of the Sad Rat."

612. ———. "The Master of Rampling Gate."

613. **Scott, Sir Walter.** "Rokeby" (excerpt).

614. **Serling, Rod.** "The Riddle of the Crypt."
A traditional kind of vampire tale but with a modern setting.
Irene and Roy rent a house on Castle Rock where legend says a vam-

pire lives. The legend turns out to be true, but Dr. Felton, a local physician in a Van Helsing-like role, helps save the day.

615. **Shakespeare, William.** "Romeo and Juliet" (excerpt).

616. **Southey, Robert.** "Thalaba the Destroyer" (excerpt).

617. **Stevenson, Robert Louis.** "Olalla."

618. **Sting.** "Moon Over Bourbon Street."

619. **Stoker, Bram.** "Dracula's Guest."

620. **Turgenev, Ivan.** "Phantoms."

621. **Verne, Jules.** "The Carpathian Castle" (excerpt).

622. **Voltaire.** "Vampires."

623. **Wells, H. G.** "The Flowering of the Strange Orchid."

624. **Wharton, Edith.** "Bewitched."

625. **Tolstoy, Alexis.** *Vampires: Stories of the Supernatural.* Edited by Linda Kuehl. Translated by Fedor Nikanov. Illustrated by Mel Fowler. New York: Hawthorn, 1969. Hardcover.
Count Alexis Constantinovich Tolstoy was author, poet, and older cousin of Count Leo Tolstoy of *War and Peace* fame. The spooky tales in this collection were written sometime in the mid-nineteenth century. Of the four stories in this collection only two have a vampire theme— "The Vampire" and "The Family of a Vourdalak."

626. ———. "The Vampire."
A young man named Runevsky becomes enamored of a beautiful girl whose grandmother, warns an acquaintance, is a vampire. This acquaintance, a man by the name of Rybarenko, tells his new friend his own horrifying tale of a vampiric encounter in order to convince Runevsky of his story's truth.

627. ———. "The Family of a Vourdalak."

In a small peasant village, the patriarch of a family returns from an outing as a vourdalak, a kind of vampire who prefers the blood of close relatives and friends.

628. ———. "Amena."
   Non-vampire theme.

629. ———. "The Reunion after Three Hundred Years."
   Non-vampire theme.

YOUNG ADULT

Some of the best stories being written today are marketed as young adult fiction. Usually the books are less than 200 pages long and have teenage protagonists. Adult readers usually pass by these books, which is a shame because these stories often offer compelling plots and well-drawn characters. One of my favorites is *Companions of the Night* by Vivian Vande Velde (*see* #659).

630. **Adams, Carmen.** *Song of the Vampire.* New York: Avon Flare, 1996. Paperback.

Teenagers Megan and Iris are sought out by an underground organization of vampire hunters because they have proven ability in spotting and dispatching these undead. The organization's contact, Derek, explains that a group of bloodsuckers is preying on a transient population of teens, mostly runaways who end up in the small town of Turo, California. The girls must seek out the undead and send them to oblivion. Things get complicated when Megan falls hard for one very charming vampire.

631. **Adams, Nicholas.** *Vampire's Kiss.* New York: HarperPaperbacks, 1994.

Weird things are happening in Galveston, Texas. Seventeen-year-old Susan Scott is haunted by the ghost of Drew Morris, who sends a warning via her television set (he was a TV journalist) that she and her friends are in danger. He is right. A band called the Blood Brothers has recently opened a club, Dark of the Moon. The boys in this band have a mesmerizing presence that hypnotizes Susan's friends Frederica and Angela. Drew uses his psychic link with this world to let Susan know that the Blood Brothers are vampires.

632. **Cooney, Caroline B.** Vampire series.

The setting for each story in the series is a dark, Victorian house with a spooky tower where the Vampire dwells.

633. ———. *The Cheerleader*. New York: Scholastic, 1991.
Series: Vampire No. 1.
Althea envies the beautiful, popular Celeste and makes a Faustian pact with the Vampire in the tower. Althea is now the popular one, but she finds she cannot enjoy her ill-gotten gains when she sees the suffering of Celeste and others.

634. ———. *The Return of the Vampire*. New York: Scholastic, 1991.
Paperback.
Series: Vampire No. 2.
The Vampire promises Devnee that she can have the beauty she desperately desires, but this promise comes at a high price. Eventually Devnee finds her conscience and also the courage to fight the evil Vampire.

635. ———. *The Vampire's Promise*. New York: Scholastic, 1993. Paperback.
Series: Vampire No. 3.
A group of teens enters the old house looking for excitement. They find it when the Vampire captures them and promises to let them go, but only after they select one from among them who will stay with him as his victim. The young people must work together to defeat this evil being.

636. **Harrell, Janice.** *Blood Curse*. New York: Scholastic, 1995. Paperback.
Series: Vampire's Love Vol. 1.
Only sixteen when she became a vampire, Rina has lived 200 years, but never really loved anyone until she met James. Things turn ugly, however, when James's girlfriend, Chelsea, becomes a vampire and seeks revenge on the new twosome.

637. ———. *Blood Spell*. New York: Scholastic, 1995. Paperback.
Series: Vampire's Love Vol. 2.
Rina and James are hunted by not only Chelsea, but also Vlad, the evil vampire who "turned" Rina 200 years ago. Meanwhile, Rina desperately wants to become human again, so James helps her seek a cure.

638. ———. Vampire Twins series.

As in so many young adult series, these books must be read in sequence and should be thought of as one story. After their mother dies, twins Paul and Anne Marie (Ari) are sent to live with their Aunt Gabrielle. Her love for them is genuine and she feels it important that they be given an appreciation of their heritage. Like Gabrielle, their father is a vampire and the twins have the natural special quality that will allow them to make the change. The twins are both horrified at first, but Paul eventually is seduced into the vampire world. This entertaining series moves at a brisk pace and has some splendid, eccentric characters.

639. ———. *Bloodlines*. New York: HarperPaperbacks, 1990. Paperback.
Series: Vampire Twins 1.

640. ———. *Bloodlust*. New York: HarperPaperbacks, 1994. Paperback.
Series: Vampire Twins 2.

641. ———. *Bloodchoice*. New York: HarperPaperbacks, 1990. Paperback.
Series: Vampire Twins 3.

642. ———. *Blood Reunion*. New York: HarperPaperbacks, 1996. Paperback.
Series: Vampire Twins 4.

643. **Pike, Christopher.** The Last Vampire series.

Beautiful Sita looks eighteen but is actually 5,000 years old. One of the first vampires created, she is now almost the last. But there is one even older than she. His name is Yaksha, and he is out to destroy her. When the series begins, Sita shows herself to be without guilt or remorse for the countless killings she has committed. Then she meets Ray, who reminds her so much of the husband she loved as a mortal. Ray aids her in her plan to find Yaksha and kill him before he can kill her. Eons ago both Sita and Yaksha made a pact with the ancient god Lord Krishna. Now they must play out the final part of their pact. And when that is done the original evil that brought vampirism to this world must be dealt with. Mixed in with a great deal of violence are dream sequences with Krishna appearing to Sita and telling her parables that, if she can figure them out, will aid her in defeating her enemies. Much of the subplot is based on the mythology of India.

644. ———. *The Last Vampire*. New York: Pocket Books (Archway Paperbacks), 1994. Paperback.
Series: The Last Vampire No. 1.

645. ———. *Black Blood*. New York: Pocket Books (Archway Paperbacks, 1994. Paperback.
Series: The Last Vampire No. 2.

646. ———. *Red Dice*. New York: Pocket Books (Archway Paperbacks), 1995. Paperback.
Series: The Last Vampire No. 3.

647. ———. *Phantom*. New York: Pocket Books (Archway Paperbacks), 1996. Paperback.
Series: The Last Vampire No. 4.

648. ———. *Evil Thirst*. New York: Pocket Books (Archway Paperbacks), 1996. Paperback.
Series: The Last Vampire No. 5.

649. ———. *Creatures of Forever*. New York: Pocket Books (Archway Paperbacks), 1996. Paperback.
Series: The Last Vampire No. 6.

650. **Plante, Edmund.** *Alone in the House*. New York: Avon, 1991. Paperback.
Joanne's parents are in Hawaii for two weeks, and she has the house to herself. Her friend Cindy talks her into throwing a big party and inviting all the popular kids. More than just invitees show up. Strangers come as well and are allowed to enter. Unfortunately, one of them turns out to be a vampire. He decides to take up residence in Joanne's house.

651. **Smith, L. J.** The Vampire Diaries Trilogy.
Stefan arrives in the small town of Fells Church (sic), Virginia. He is lonely and different. A vampire, he puts himself into a world of normals by attending the local high school. He survives on animal blood

and avoids the human variety even though it would enhance his vampiric powers. Stefan finds himself attracted to the lovely, popular Elena; however, he tries to keep away from her because she reminds him so much of Katherine, the woman who centuries ago turned him and his brother Damon into immortals. Shortly after Stefan's arrival in town, some mysterious murders occur. The victims are drained of blood. Elena discovers the truth about Stefan, and she also finds out that Damon is in the vicinity. Damon and Stefan have been enemies since their rebirth as vampires and the apparent true death of Katherine, whom they both loved.

652. ———. *The Awakening*. New York: HarperPaperbacks, 1991. Paperback.
Series: The Vampire Diaries Vol. 1.

653. ———. *The Struggle*. New York: HarperPaperbacks, 1991. Paperback.
Series: The Vampire Diaries Vol. 2.

654. ———. *The Fury*. New York: HarperPaperbacks, 1991. Paperback.
Series: The Vampire Diaries Vol. 3.

655. ———. *Dark Reunion*. New York: HarperPaperbacks, 1992. Paperback.
Series: The Vampire Diaries Vol. 4.
In this sequel to the trilogy, Elena summons Stefan and Damon to help defeat a terrible evil that has come to Fells Church. They discover that a vampiric entity—one of the Old Ones—is behind the recent death of a student and other terrible deeds.

656. ———. *Secret Vampire*. New York: Archway Paperbacks, 1996. Paperback.
Publisher Series: Night World.
Werewolves, vampires, and witches populate the Night World. Humans are referred to as vermin. Elders make the draconian rules that Night People must live by. Members may not fall in love with a human nor may they reveal the existence of this secret world.
Poppy has just finished her junior year of high school when she discovers she has incurable pancreatic cancer. Her friend James belongs

to the Night World. He reveals his vampiric nature to Poppy and offers to save her by transforming her into a vampire. He makes this offer knowing that by doing so he endangers himself. The consequences for an unauthorized transformation of a human is death. James has broken all the Night World rules for Poppy because he loves her. She decides to accept his offer.

657. ——. *Soulmate*. New York: Archway Paperbacks, 1997. Paperback.

Publisher series: Night World.

Hannah thinks she might be going crazy. She keeps finding notes in her own handwriting with strange, scary messages like "Dead before seventeen" and "He's coming." She is frightened and doesn't know what to do. She isn't crazy, of course; she has come up against the Night World. Thousands of years ago she became the love of Thierry, the first vampire created by Maya. Because of a curse their love has been doomed throughout Hannah's numerous reincarnations. Thierry vows to break the dark cycle this time around.

658. ——. *The Chosen*. New York: Archway Paperbacks, 1997. Paperback.

Publisher series: Night World.

As a child of five Rashel Jordan watched a vampire kill her mother. Then the vampire goes after Rashel, but even at this tender age, she is a survivor. With a force of will she turns off the vampire's telepathic pull and escapes. Now at age seventeen she is a vampire killer who finishes off any that she finds with a special Japanese sword made of wood. Her perspective on the undead changes when she meets Quinn, a vampire for more than four hundred years. It takes an adventure involving a slave trade in teenage girls before the two realize they are truly soulmates.

659. **Vande Velde, Vivian.** *Companions of the Night*. New York: Laurel-Leaf, 1995.

Kerry is sixteen and still suffering over her mother's recent abandonment. Late one evening, at the local laundry, she walks into a nightmare scenario. A young man, Ethan, has been beaten and gagged by a group of four men who accuse him of being a vampire. She does not believe such nonsense and, at the first opportunity, helps Ethan to escape. But it turns out that Ethan really is one of the undead. Now Kerry has to make some adult decisions as she tries to figure out where the true evil lies—with the vampire or with his hunters.

660. **William, Kate (writer), and Francine Pascal (creator).**
Sweet Valley High Vampire Trilogy.
Jessica Wakefield believes she and Sweet Valley High's new student, Jonathan Cain, are soulmates, but her friend, Enid, feels the same way about him. In fact, many are attracted to this dark, moody stranger. Elizabeth, Jessica's identical twin, is one of the few to sense that Jonathan is dangerous. Her concern for her sister's desperate passion turns to genuine fear when blood-drained bodies begin showing up around town.

661. ———. *Tall, Dark, and Deadly*. New York: Bantam, 1996. Paperback.
Series: Sweet Valley High Vampire Trilogy No. 1.
Publisher series: Sweet Valley High No. 126.

662. ———. *Dance of Death*. New York: Bantam, 1996. Paperback.
Series: Sweet Valley High Vampire Trilogy No. 2.
Publisher series: Sweet Valley High No. 127.

663. ———. *Kiss of a Killer*. New York: Bantam, 1996. Paperback
Series: Sweet Valley High Vampire Trilogy No. 3.
Publisher series: Sweet Valley High No. 128.

ADDITIONAL READINGS

This section contains books that explain the vampire myth, discuss the literature of the vampire genre, or give historic analysis of personages such as Vlad Tepes or Elizabeth Bathory who have inspired the stories of the immortal undead.

664. **Auerbach, Nina.** *Our Vampires, Ourselves.* Chicago: University of Chicago Press, 1995. Hardcover. (Paperback. University of Chicago Press, 1995.)

In her introduction Auerbach notes that "vampires go where power is." Thus, she begins her analysis of vampire fiction with stories that sprang from writers in nineteenth-century Britain and then moves on to vampires as seen through America's twentieth-century prism. This is an academic approach to literature and films, but one that will interest all aficionados of the genre.

665. **Bontly, Susan, and Carol J. Sheridan.** *Enchanted Journeys Beyond the Imagination: An Annotated Bibliography of Fantasy, Futuristic, Supernatural and Time Travel Romances.* Beavercreek, OH: Blue Diamond Publications, 1996. Paperback. In 3 volumes.

A bibliography containing brief annotations of various category romance subgenres including vampires.

666. **Carter, Margaret L. (editor).** *The Vampire in Literature: A Critical Bibliography.* Ann Arbor, MI: UMI Research Press, 1989. Paperback.

The initial chapters give a survey of vampire literature and explore the legends behind the stories. The remaining chapters are bibliographic listings under the following headings: Vampire Fiction in

English (the largest section); Anthologies of Vampire Fiction and Verse; Non-English Vampire Fiction in Translation; Dramatic Works on Vampires in English; Nonfiction: Books; Nonfiction: Articles. The fiction entries have abbreviations that designate what sort of vampiric creature the reader may expect to encounter. For example A1H means a vampire who is Alien, Humanoid. Annual updates are available from the editor.

667. **Cox, Greg.** *The Transylvanian Library: A Consumer's Guide to Vampire Fiction.* San Bernardino, CA: Borgo Press, 1993. Hardcover.
   In this bibliography of vampire fiction, witty annotations by Greg Cox make for lively reading about the undead. Beginning with the pre-Dracula stories like Polidori's *The Vampyre,* readers are treated to a chronological exploration of vampire fiction up to 1989. Cox is wonderfully opinionated and uses a rating system of one to four bats. Says Cox, "When I finally closed the door of this Library, *The Queen of the Damned (see* #204) had just seen print and Ronald Reagan was still president. Since then I have seen the vampire boom of the 1980s go thermonuclear."

668. **Farson, Daniel.** *The Man Who Wrote Dracula: A Biography of Bram Stoker.* New York: St. Martin's, 1975. Hardcover.
   The great-nephew of Bram Stoker has written an entertaining account of his famous ancestor. Stoker loved the theater and gave up a safe civil service job to manage the career of the actor Sir Henry Irving as well as handle the business affairs of the Lyceum Theatre. A man of tremendous energy, he was able, during this same time, to obtain a degree in law and to write. But of course much of this book is devoted to the fictional Dracula and the evil Vlad Tepes, who may have been the inspiration for Stoker's most famous character.

669. **Gordon, Joan, and Veronica Hollinger (editors).** *Blood Read: The Vampire as Metaphor in Contemporary Culture.* Philadelphia: University of Pennsylvania Press, 1997.
   This collection of fourteen essays focuses on the role of the vampire as metaphor in contemporary culture. It explores this aspect of the conventional horror figure in recent fiction and film and to some extent in television and comic books. The foreward is by Brian Aldiss; fiction writers Suzy McKee Charnas, Jewelle Gomez, and Brian Stableford

have written about their own work; and scholars from the United States, Canada, and Japan, among them Nina Auerbach, Margaret Carter, Rob Tatham, and Mari Kotani, have contributed essays.

670. **Hoyt, Olga.** *Lust for Blood: The Consuming Story of Vampires.* Chelsea, MI: Scarborough House, 1984. Hardcover and paperback.

A modern-day aspiring vampire was a dapper Englishman named John Haigh, who first charmed his victims, then killed them with a blow to the head, after which he drained their blood and robbed their estates. Thus begins Hoyt's account of vampires throughout history—those who inspired the legend such as Haigh, Countess Elizabeth Bathory, and Vlad Tepes, as well as their fictional counterparts Dracula, Varney, and Carmilla, to name a few. A look at the cultures that inspired the legends of such fiends gives a background to the discussion of the tales themselves.

671. **McNally, Raymond T., and Radu Florescu.** *Dracula: A Biography of Vlad the Impaler, 1431–1476.* New York: Hawthorn, 1973. Hardcover.

Using primary sources, such as Vlad Tepes' correspondence and other documents, the authors piece together a fascinating (and gruesome) account of this warrior prince whose cruelty was noted even in an age when torture was considered a normal tool of interrogation. Detailed chapter notes and an excellent bibliography follow the text.

672. ———. *In Search of Dracula: A True History of Dracula and Vampire Legends.* New York: Galahad Books, 1972. Hardcover.

The publication of this book by two historians linked the Wallachian Prince Vlad Tepes (also known as Dracula) with Bram Stoker's vampiric count. This popular history gives an intriguing account of Vlad's horrific rule and makes the case for how and why Stoker used this historical personage as the evil protagonist of his novel.

673. ———. *In Search of Dracula: The History of Dracula and Vampires.* Boston: Houghton Mifflin, 1994. Paperback. Completely revised edition.

In this new edition the authors have had the advantage of access to recently discovered, unpublished journals that Stoker used while composing *Dracula*. Other research, some aided by the fall of the Iron Curtain, gives more substance to the connection between the historical and literary Dracula. Included is a bibliography of vampire fiction and nonfiction as well as an annotated filmography.

674. **Melton, J. Gordon.** *The Vampire Book: The Encyclopedia of the Undead.* Detroit, MI: Visible Ink Press, 1994.

An excellent reference source that covers many aspects of vampire literature, myth and culture. It is an encyclopedic approach with essays on subjects such as Lord Byron, *Dark Shadows*, characteristics of vampires, the Highgate Vampire, and vampire myths around the world. There is also a bibliography of novels, a filmography, and even a list of organizations devoted to the undead.

675. **Ramsland, Katherine.** *The Anne Rice Reader: Writers Explore the Universe of Anne Rice.* New York: Ballantine, 1997. Paperback.

Anne Rice's biographer, Katherine Ramsland, has put together a collection of essays and articles about Rice and her works. Two early short stories by Rice are also included. Literary critiques include "The World of the Vampire" by Gail Abbott Zimmerman, "Lestat: The Vampire as Degenerate Genius" by Richard Noll, and "He Must Have Wept When He Made You: The Homoerotic Pathos in the Movie Version of *Interview with the Vampire*" by John Beebe.

676. ———. *The Vampire Companion: The Official Guide to Anne Rice's The Vampire Chronicles.* New York: Ballantine, 1993. Hardcover.

The essays in this first edition cover the first four books of the Chronicles (*see* #202–205). Book five, *Memnoch the Devil*, had not yet been published.

677. ———. *The Vampire Companion: The Official Guide to Anne Rice's The Vampire Chronicles.* New York: Ballantine, 1995. Paperback. Completely revised and updated edition.

This companion piece compiled by Rice biographer Ramsland is an excellent resource for those who enjoyed the rich tapestry of Rice's Vampire Chronicles (*see* #202–206). The encyclopedic format includes essays on every character, place, imagery, plot line, literary allusion, and significant event that appears in each of the five books that make up the Chronicles. Also included are essays on *The Witching Hour*—book one of the Mayfair Witches series. An added attraction is a short story by Rice which became the basis for *Interview with the Vampire*.

678. **Rein-Hagen, Mark.** *Book of the Kindred.* Clarkston, GA: White Wolf, 1996. Paperback.
This book was published to appear in conjunction with the now defunct TV series *Kindred: The Embraced*. Still, it is a good source for readers of White Wolf's World of Darkness: Vampire novels. The chapters concentrate on giving background information about the Kindred (vampires), their origins, clan structure and differences, and social status. There is a lexicon which can be very useful to anyone new to the World of Darkness. Short stories of the Kindred are also included: "Smoke" by Don Bassingthwaite, "Eye of the Beholder" by Lawrence Watt-Evans, "Reconciliation" by Matt Forbeck, and "Ruins" by Jim Morre.

679. ———. *Vampire: The Masquerade: A Storytelling Game of Personal Horror.* Clarkston, GA: White Wolf, 1992. Hardcover.
This book is aimed primarily for those involved in White Wolf's role-playing game Vampire: The Masquerade. The first section will also be of interest to readers of the World of Darkness series since it describes the nature of the vampire or Kindred, the various social distinctions, the laws governing those who have been Embraced, the various clans, and a brief discussion of other creatures that inhabit this alternate universe. The major sections of this book give details on a variety of role-playing games and how best to play them.

680. **Skal, David J.** *V Is for Vampire: The A-Z Guide to Everything Undead.* New York: Plume, 1996. Paperback.
The subtitle to the contrary, this book does not quite cover everything to do with the undead; however, it has interesting information on all things vampiric. The real emphasis of this book, though, is film. Skal's passion for vampire movies shows through in his delightfully opinionated essays.

THE UNREAD UNDEAD

There are so many books (novels, anthologies, critical essays, etc.) featuring the vampire that it is impossible to list them all. In this final section is a gathering of titles that I would like to have found, read, and included with full annotations, but that was not always possible. In preparing the unread list I have relied on reviews, publisher catalogs, trade publications, fanzines, and recommendations from colleagues. For most of these titles I have been able to give some idea of what they are about and put them in their proper categories. For some titles a bit of guesswork was needed.

As I look through the pages of journals such as *Locus* and *Publishers Weekly* I find more and more books on publishers' forthcoming lists. When the unread become read and the as-yet-unpublished transform into real books they will appear, with annotations, at the Internet Web Site for Vampire Readings:

http://www.bibliography.com/vamp/

Readers are encouraged to contact me via e-mail at:

infoseek@bibliography.com

Unread Novels

681. **Angeleno.** *A Working Class Vampire Is Something To Be.* Seattle, WA: Ice Dragon Ltd. (P.O. Box 17464, Seattle, WA 98107-1164), 1992.

College dropout Mike Teller attends a Halloween party, takes too many drugs, meets some strange people, and at sunset of All Souls' Day wakes up as a vampire.

682. **Armstrong, F. W.** *The Devouring.* New York: Tor, 1987.

A plague is unleashed on humanity causing those afflicted to turn into vampires and other monsters.

683. **Ashley, Amanda.** *A Darker Dream.* New York: Love Spell, 1997.
A romance novel featuring the handsome, brooding, wealthy vampire, Lord Rayven who finds love and redemption with the beautiful Rhianna.

684. **Baker, Nancy.** *Blood and Chrysanthemums.* (Canada): Penguin, 1995.
This sequel to *The Night Inside (see #9)* continues the adventures of Ardeth and Dimitri.

685. **Bassingthwaite, Don, and Nancy Kilpatrick.** *As One Dead.* Clarkson, GA: White Wolf, 1996.
Publisher series: World of Darkness: Vampire.
In Toronto the vampire association Sabbat reigns supreme but a rival group, the Camarilla, attempts a rebellion. A Romeo-and-Juliet plot unfolds as Bianka and Lot, from opposing clans, fall in love.

686. **Byers, Richard Lee.** *The Vampire's Apprentice.* New York: Zebra, 1992.
David is a loser who joins a New Age study group hoping to make his life better. Instead the group's leader tricks him into becoming a vampire—a way of life even more difficult and horrendous than David ever imagined.

687. **Carr, A. A.** *Eye Killers.* University of Oklahoma Press, 1995.
This unusual tale is told from the perspective of a Native American. Melissa, the teenage granddaughter of Michael Roanhorse, encounters the vampire Falke. Michael and Melissa's teacher team up to save the girl.

688. **Cecilione, Michael.** *Domination.* New York: Zebra, 1993.
A reporter becomes entangled in a feud between two ancient, powerful vampires. As the title indicates, there is quite a bit of sadomasochism.

689. **Cervello, Mike.** *The Refuge of Night: A Modern Vampire Myth with a Bonus Tale of Renaissance Terror.* Elmhurst, New York: C V K Publishing, 1996.
Lena Banks is a vampire and FBI agent. Her first case is to track

down a serial killer. Also included in this volume is a short story—the bonus tale—about a female immortal pursued by a vampire hunter.

690. **Chilton, Athan Y.** *Try Catching Cat.* Mason, MI: Bill Hupe and Peg Kennedy, Footrot Flats, 916 Lamb Road, Mason, MI 48854-9445, 1994.
Paul and Callina are vampires and lovers on the run from other members of the undead who want these two to meet their final death.

691. **Ciencin, Scott.** *Blood Kiss.* New York: Zebra, May 1997.

692. **Collins, Nancy A.** *Walking Wolf: A Weird Western.* Shingletown, CA: Mark V. Ziesing, 1995.
This novel features a vampire gunslinger.

693. **Courtney, Vincent.** *Harvest of Blood.* New York: Pinnacle, 1992. Series: Christopher Blaze No. 2.
This is a sequel to *Vampire Beat* (*see* #47) with former policeman and vampire Chris Blaze now a private investigator. In this story he looks into the disappearance of a onetime assistant district attorney.

694. **Dvorkin, David.** *Unquenchable.* New York: Zebra, 1995.
This is a sequel to *Insatiable* (*see* #63). Richard Venneman has regained his humanity, but now wishes for those lost vampiric powers.

695. **Freed, L. A.** *Blood Thirst.* New York: Pinnacle Books, 1989.

696. **Gallagher, Stephen.** *Morningstar.* New York: Ballantine, 1993.

697. **Garrett, Susan M.** *Forever Knight: Intimations of Mortality.* New York: Boulevard, November 1997.
This novel is based on the TV show about the vampire homicide detective Nick Knight. Here Nick's continuing quest for mortality brings him into contact with a mysterious woman who promises to grant his wish.

698. **Gideon, John.** *Golden Eyes.* New York: Berkley, 1994.
The narrator of this suspenseful tale learns he has some vampire relatives.

699. ———. *Greeley's Cove.* New York: Jove, 1991.

700. **Graverson, Pat.** *Sweet Blood*. New York: Zebra, 1992.
    Series: Adragon Hart No. 1.
    Seventeen-year-old Adragon finds there are some advantages and quite a few disadvantages to being a vampire. His girlfriend, his mother, and the Society of Vampires contrive to make his new unlife difficult.

701. ———. *Precious Blood*. New York: Zebra, 1993.
    Series: Adragon Hart No. 2.
    In this sequel to *Sweet Blood* (*see* #700) Adragon is now married and the father of Beth, who has inherited the vampiric trait.

702. **Griffith, Kathryn Meyer.** *Vampire Blood*. New York: Zebra, 1992.
    A family of vampires moves into town and sets up their home in a once-opulent movie theater. Of course it isn't obvious at first just what these creatures are, but soon enough the heroine, Jenny, discovers the truth.

703. **Hodge, Brian.** *Shrines and Desecrations*. Leesburg, VA: TAL, 1994.

704. **Johnson, V. M.** *Dhampir, Child of the Blood*. (POB 1036/SM) Fairfield, Conn. 06432: Mystic Rose Books, 1997.
    How to raise a dhampir (child of a vampire), from a mother's perspective.

705. **Kemske, Floyd.** *Human Resources: A Corporate Nightmare*. Catbird Press, 1995.
    This is a satiric look at the corporate world wherein one major company is really and truly run by a bloodsucker.

706. **Kilpatrick, Nancy.** See #742A under Unread Anthologies.

707. **Lake, Paul.** *Among the Immortals*. Brownsville, OR: Story Line Press, 1994.
    Student Derek Hill discovers the dark and seamy side of academia after his favorite professor is murdered by a psychotic—or maybe the man isn't crazy after all.

708. **Lee, Tanith.** *Vivia*. Little Brown, 1995.

Vivia, the daughter of a noble, flees a plague and hides in a cave. There she encounters a vampire who offers her immortality.

709. **Lisle, Holly.** *Hunting the Corrigan's Blood.* Riverdale, New York: Baen, 1997.
Cadence Drake is hired to find a stolen spaceship. Unfortunately the trail leads her and her partner into the path of unmitigated evil.

710. **Lowder, James.** *The Screaming Tower.* Lake Geneva, WI: TSR, 1991.

711. **Martindale, T. Chris.** *Nightblood.* New York: Warner, 1990.
Chris is a Vietnam vet whose brother Alex has been brutally murdered. Alex's ghost will not let Chris rest until he tracks down the killer. This leads Chris into a nest of vampires.

712. **Moore, James, and Kevin Murphy.** *House of Secrets.* Clarkston, GA: White Wolf, 1995.
Publisher series: World of Darkness: Vampire.
Etrius, mage and vampire, plans a ceremony that will return him to human status and transform the universe into a place hostile to the undead.

713. **Morgan, Robert.** *Some Things Never Die.* New York: Diamond, 1993.
A woman asks private investigator Teddy London to find the vampires that killed her son. London is skeptical, naturally, but he soon discovers that beings such as these really do exist.

714. **Morton, Gary.** *Channelling the Vampire.* Toronto: Grim Commander Press, 1994.
The vampire Count Titus Varsook has a stake driven through his heart, but instead of meeting his final death, his spirit takes residence in the body of Jon Chandler, con man and fake channeller.

715. **Muss-Barnes, Eric.** *The Gothic Rainbow.* Brooklyn, OH: Dubh Sith Ink, 1997.
Series: The Vampire Noctuaries 1.

The vampire narrator of this story tells his tale in a stream-of-consciousness style.

716. **Neiderman, Andrew.** *The Need.* New York: Putnam's, 1992.
     Richard and Clea are vampires but they inhabit one body. When Richard kills Clea's lover she vows revenge.

717. **Petersen, Gail.** *The Making of a Monster.* New York: Dell/Abyss, 1993.
     Before moving from New York to Los Angeles, Kate was a conventional woman in a conventional marriage. Then she meets Justin, who transforms her from human to a monster who must kill for blood or die.

718. **Ryan, Shawn.** *Nocturnas.* New York: Pocket Books, 1995.
     An American journalist discovers that a band of former Romanian secret police are an especially vicious breed of vampire who have recently teamed up with a drugs and arms smuggler.

719. **Saberhagen, Fred.** *Dominion.* New York: Tor, 1982.
     Series: Dracula No. 5.
     In this Dracula adventure, the vampire count meets Merlin and finds himself hurled back to the time of Camelot (*see* #213–221 for other titles in the series).

720. **Saberhagen, Fred, and James V. Hart.** *Bram Stoker's Dracula: A Francis Ford Coppola Film. Based on the Screenplay by James V. Hart; From the Bram Stoker Novel.* New York: Signet, 1992.
     In Coppola's spin on the Dracula story, we are given a reason for the Count's transformation to immortal and for his obsession with Mina.

721. **Sargent, Carl, and Marc Gasciogne.** *Nosferatu.* New York: Penguin ROC, 1994.
     This novel is set in the world of Shadowrun, a role-playing game. Among the many paranormal characters in this story is Luther, a mad scientist as well as vampire.

722. **Sizemore, Susan.** *Forever Knight: A Stirring of Dust.* New York: Boulevard, 1997.
     Another Nick Knight story (*see* #697). Nick suspects that the brutal killer of four decapitated victims may be one of his own kind—a vampire.

723. **Spinrad, Norman.** *Vampire Junkies.* Brooklyn, NY: Gryphon Books, 1994.
Count Dracula arrives in New York City and promptly quenches his thirst at the throat of a heroin-addicted prostitute. As a result, both of them enjoy getting high on drugs and druggies.

724. **Stableford, Brian N.** *The Hunger and Ecstasy of Vampires.* Shingletown, CA: Mark V. Ziesing (P.O. Box 76, Shingletown, CA 96088), 1996.
At a gathering of Victorian notables, Professor Edward Copplestone tells of a personal adventure in which he has traveled to a far future where vampires reign supreme over humans.

725. **Stine, R. L.** *Goodnight Kiss.* New York: Archway/Pocket, 1992.
Jessica and Gabriel meet on a blind date and find, to their surprise, that each is a vampire.

725A. **Talbot, Michael.** *The Delicate Dependency: A Novel of the Vampire Life.* New York: Avon, 1982.
While searching for his kidnapped daughter, Victorian-era scientist Dr. John Gladstone comes across the hidden world of the vampire.

726. **Tilton, Lois.** *Vampire Winter.* New York: Pinnacle, 1990.
Blaine Kittredge's existence as a vampire changes radically after a nuclear attack. Now he and the human survivors must find a way to work together.

727. **Weathersby, Lee.** *Kiss of the Vampire.* New York: Zebra, 1992.
Good guy vampire Simon and the mortal woman he loves are being hunted by a savage bunch of immortals led by Simon's crazed, evil brother.

728. **Weinberg, Robert.** *The Armageddon Box.* New York: Leisure, 1991.
The vampires first entered our world when a sorcerer of Atlantis opened the gates to the Land of Shadow. These evil beings are locked in a battle with mortals and modern mages for a book that will give its owner great power.

729. **Whitten, Leslie.** *The Fangs of the Morning.* New York: Leisure, 1994.
   A killer dubbed the Vampire of the Mall gets his fangs into a homicide detective who doesn't let transformation to undead status stop him from hunting his quarry.

730. **Wilde, Kelley.** *Mastery.* New York: Dell, 1991.
   The passage of Halley's comet causes a time-travel reaction that sends a group of people from 1986 back to 1906. One of them is a vampire.

731. **Williams, Tad, and Nina Kiriki Hoffman.** *Child of an Ancient City.* New York: Tor, 1994.
   This tale has an Arabian Nights flavor. A group of travelers wanders into a vampire's domain. To save themselves at least one of them must tell a story that is sadder than the vampire's own.

732. **Williamson, Chet.** *Mordenheim.* Lake Geneva, WI: TSR, 1994.

733. **Williamson, J. N.** *Bloodlines.* Stanford, CT: Longmeadow, 1994.
   Marshall is a psychotic vampire who will stop at nothing to find his two children and introduce them to their "proper heritage."

734. **Wilson, David Niall.** *To Sift Through Bitter Ashes.* Clarkston, GA: White Wolf, 1997.
   Series: The Grails Covenant Book One.
   Publisher series: World of Darkness: Vampire: The Dark Ages.
   During the time of the Crusades the vampire Montrovant enters Jerusalem in search of the Holy Grail.

735. **Wright, T. Lucien.** *Blood Brothers.* New York: Pinnacle, 1992.
   In a small town in upstate New York, the creeping presence of the vampire makes itself known.

Unread Anthologies and Novellas

736. **Bennett, Janice, Sara Blayne, and Monique Ellis.** *Lords of the Night.* New York: Zebra, 1997.
   Three romantic vampire tales set in Regency England.

737. **Cox, Greg, and T. K. F. Weisskopf (editors).** *Tomorrow Sucks.* New York: Baen, 1994.

   Eleven SF vampire tales. In these stories (all reprints) vampirism has a scientific explanation.

738. **Dalby, Richard (editor).** *Dracula's Brood.* New York: Barnes & Noble, 1996.

   A collection of rarely reprinted vampire stories. All were written between the years 1867 and 1940.

739. ————. *Vampire Stories.* Seacaucus, NJ: Castle Books, 1993.

   A conventional mixture of vampire tales, most of which are reprints. There is a foreword by actor Peter Cushing.

740. **Dziemianowicz, Stefan R., Robert Weinberg, and Martin H. Greenberg (editors).** *Virtuous Vampires.* New York: Barnes & Noble, 1996.

   As the title indicates, the undead in these stories show that vampire guys and gals can be benevolent, even altruistic.

741. **Gladwell, Adele Olivia, and Richard Havoc (editors).** *Blood & Roses: The Vampire in Nineteenth Century Literature.* London: Creation Press, 1992. (U.S. distributor: Inland Book Co., 140 Commerce St., East Haven, CT 06512.)

   A sampling of nineteenth-century stories with vampiric themes.

742. **Greenberg, Martin H. (editor).** *Dracula: Prince of Darkness.* New York: DAW, 1992.

   An anthology of original stories in which modern-day writers such as F. Paul Wilson and P. N. Elrod use Stoker's famous count as their protagonist.

742A. **Kilpatrick, Nancy.** *Sex and the Single Vampire.* Leesburg, VA: TAL, 1994.

743. **King, Valerie.** "The Vampire Rogue." In *Bewitched by Love.* New York: Zebra, 1996.

744. **Knight, Amarantha (editor).** *Love Bites.* New York: Masquerade, 1995.

This volume of vampire tales focuses on the sexual charms and erotic allure of blood-drinking immortals. Authors include Ron Dee, Nancy A. Collins, Nancy Kilpatrick, and Lois Tilton.

745. **Kramer, Edward E. (editor).** *Dark Destiny III: Children of Dracula.* Clarkston, GA: White Wolf, 1996.
   Publisher series: World of Darkness.
   Twenty-one original stories, most of which are set in White Wolf's World of Darkness milieu and several featuring the famous count.

746. **Krause, Stanley, and Stewart Wieck.** *Strange City.* New York: HarperPrism, 1996.
   Publisher series: World of Darkness: Vampire.
   This collection includes tales of all the exotic predators—vampires, wraiths, mages, and werewolves—that inhabit the World of Darkness.

747. **Tan, Cecilia (editor).** *Blood Kiss.* Cambridge, MA: Circlet Press, 1994.
   A collection of seven erotic stories including an "out-take" from the novel *Diary of a Vampire* by Gary Bowen (*see* #23).

748. ———. *Erotica Vampirica.* Cambridge, MA: Circlet Press, 1996.
   A second collection of erotic tales (ten in all) about highly sexed vampires from editor Celia Tan (see #747).

749. **Weinberg, Robert, Stefan R. Dziemianowicz, and Martin H. Greenberg (editors).** *Rivals of Dracula.* New York: Barnes & Noble, 1996.
   More stories with Count Dracula as the central character. All are reprints.

750. ———. *Weird Vampire Tales.* New York: Gramercy, 1992.

Unread Young Adult Fiction

751. **Anderson, M. T.** *Thirsty.* Candlewick, 1997.

752. **Baron, Nick.** *Castle of the Undead.* Lake Geneva, WI: TSR, 1994.

Series: *Endless Quest.*

Set in TSR's Ravenloft universe, this novel allows the reader to make alternative choices as the main character, Randar, tries to escape the clutches of the vampire Vekaarn.

753. **Cooper, Molly (editor).** *Classic Vampire Stories: Timeless Tales to Sink Your Teeth Into.* Los Angeles: Lowell House Juvenile, 1996.

754. **Dokey, Cameron.** *Eternally Yours.* New York: Z-Fave, 1994.
Series: The Nightmare Club.
A handsome young vampire tries to seduce the lonely Mercy, but her suspicious best friend vows to save her.

755. **Garth, C. G.** *Bad Dog.* New York: Bantam, 1995.
Vampire Phil Bateman acquires an experimental, genetically engineered dog that eats animal remains. Then the experiment goes bad.

756. **Hoh, Diana.** *The Vampire's Kiss.* New York: Scholastic, 1995.
Publisher Series: Nightmare Hall 22.
Janie suspects that her murdered boyfriend has returned as one of the undead.

757. **Klause, Annette Curtis.** *The Silver Kiss.* New York: Delacorte, 1990.
Nice-guy vampire Simon tracks down an evil nosferatu, Christopher, who has the face and body of a sweet, innocent child.

758. **Locke, Joseph.** *Deadly Relations.* New York: Bantam, 1994.
Series: Blood & Lace.
Sequel to *Vampire Heart* (see #759).

759. ———. *Vampire Heart.* New York: Bantam, 1994.
Series: Blood & Lace.
Sabrina discovers that her weird Uncle Vikto wants to turn her into a vampire the day she turns eighteen.

760. **Pine, Nicholas.** *Night School.* New York: Berkley, 1994.
Series: Terror Academy.
Two vampire brothers, one good and one evil, fight for the affection of pretty high school student Stacey.

761. **Smith, L. J.** *Daughters of Darkness.* New York: Archway Paperback, 1996.
Publisher Series: Night World.
Three vampire sisters flee the Night World in order to live like normals, but the family sends their brother Ash to bring them back into the fold. (*See* #656–658 for other books by Smith in this series.)

Unread Additional Readings

762. **Auerbach, Nina, and David J. Skal (editors).** *Dracula: Authoritative Text, Contexts, Reviews and Reactions, Dramatic and Film Variations, Criticism.* New York: Norton, 1997.

763. **Barber, Paul.** *Vampires, Burial, and Death: Folklore and Reality.* New Haven: Yale University Press, 1988.
A sometimes ghoulish, often witty, look at the restless undead. The author uses modern science to explain the origins of the vampire myth.

764. **Belford, Barbara.** *Bram Stoker: A Biography of the Author of Dracula.* New York: Knopf, 1996.
This biography explores the theory that Stoker's employer, the actor Henry Irving, was the inspiration for Dracula.

765. **Carter, Margaret L. (editor).** *Dracula: The Vampire and the Critics.* Ann Arbor, MI: UMI Research Press, 1988.
A collection of critical essays about Stoker's classic novel.

766. **Florescu, Radu, and Raymond T. McNally.** *Dracula, Prince of Many Faces: His Life and Times.* New York: Little Brown, 1989.

767. **Gelder, Ken.** *Reading the Vampire.* New York: Routledge, 1994.
An academic analysis of the vampire genre and how it fits into the popular imagination.

768. **Guiley, Rosemary Ellen, and J. B. Macabre.** *The Complete Vampire Companion: Legend and Lore of the Living Dead.* New York: Macmillan, 1994.

A popular-style look at the vampire scene in movies, television, music, and books.

769. **Mascetti, Manuela Dunn.** *Vampire: The Complete Guide to the World of the Undead.* New York: Viking, 1992.
An exploration of the vampire myth through text and illustrations.

770. **McNally, Raymond T.** *Dracula Was a Woman.* New York: Mc-Graw-Hill, 1983.
A biography of Countess Elizabeth Bathory and how her decadent life—she murdered close to seven hundred young women—has influenced the vampire legend.

771. **Ramsland, Katherine.** *Prism of the Night: A Biography of Anne Rice.* New York: Dutton, 1991.
A biography of the author of the Vampire Chronicles (*see* #202–206).

772. **Riccardo, Martin V.** *Liquid Dreams of Vampires.* St. Paul, MN: Llewellyn, 1996.
A look at our fascination with these erotic immortals by exploring the dreams, nightmares, and fantasies of various men and women.

773. **Shepard, Leslie.** *The Book of Dracula.* Milford, CT: Outlet, 1991.

774. **Silver, Alain, and James Ursini.** *The Vampire Film: From Nosferatu to Bram Stoker's Dracula.* New York: Limelight Editions, 1993.
A critical analysis of vampire genre films.

775. **Skal, David J.** *Hollywood Gothic: The Tangled Web of "Dracula" from Novel to Stage to Screen.* New York: Norton, 1990.
An account of how the hideous monster of Stoker's novel became the seductive charmer of stage and screen.

776. **Summers, Montague.** *The Vampire in Europe.* New York: Gramercy Books, 1994.
This is a reprint of a book originally published in 1928. Summers believed in the reality of vampires. Here he has collected accounts of

what he considered true-life encounters with the undead throughout various European countries.

777. ———. *The Vampire: His Kith and Kin*. New Hyde Park, New York: University Books, 1960.
A reprint of a 1929 publication that thoroughly examines vampire folklore. As in *The Vampire in Europe* Summers writes from the perspective of a true believer in the undead.

778. **Timpone, Anthony (editor).** *Fangoria: Vampires*. New York: HarperPrism, 1996.
A collection of twenty-six articles from the pages of the horror magazine *Fangoria*. The emphasis is on movies, but there are also articles on novelists such as Anne Rice and Brian Lumley.

779. **Wolf, Leonard.** *Dracula: The Connoisseur's Guide*. New York: Broadway, 1997.
Essays by Wolf on the myth of the vampire, Bram Stoker's Dracula, and the movies and books inspired by the undead count.

AUTHOR/EDITOR INDEX

Numbers following the author or editor name refer to bibliographic entries, not pages.

TITLE INDEX

All numbers refer to bibliographic entries, not pages.

ABOUT THE AUTHOR

Patricia Altner received a BA degree from the University of Akron and an MSLS degree from the University of Kentucky. For one year she was a Lincoln-Juarez Fellow in Mexico City where she compiled a bibliography entitled *Texas and the War between the United States and Mexico* from documents in the Lafragua Collection of the National Library of Mexico. She has worked as a reference librarian at Cleveland Public Library and in various government libraries such as National Defense University and Defense Intelligence Agency.

Bibliography has always been one of the things she enjoyed most as a librarian. This book has allowed her to bring that together with her passion for vampires. She is a freelance writer and researcher who lives in Bowie, Maryland, with her husband and son.